By the author of the hilarious best-seller, NOW HEAR THIS! *

Daniel V. Gallery

CLEAR THE DECKS

"As an action-packed account of a baby flattop's campaign against U-boats in World War II, this is a corker. The author writes with warmth, understanding, clarity and rough humor." —*St. Louis Post Dispatch*

"A good deal more than a series of belly-laughs."
—*BOMC News*

"You do not need to be a lover of the sea to enjoy this splendid and humorous book." —*Columbus Dispatch*

"A RIP-SNORTING ACCOUNT!" —*Los Angeles Mirror*

* Paperback Library Book #53-980, 60¢

CLEAR THE DECKS!

Daniel V. Gallery

Rear Admiral, U. S. Navy (Ret.)

PAPERBACK LIBRARY, Inc.

New York

PAPERBACK LIBRARY EDITION

First Printing: *February, 1967*
Second Printing: *January, 1968*

Grateful acknowledgment is made to Mrs. George Bambridge, to Doubleday and Company, New York, and to The Macmillan Company of Canada Limited for permission to quote from "McAndrew's Hymn" from *The Seven Seas*, by Rudyard Kipling; and to the Macmillan Company, New York, for permission to quote from *Sea Fever*, by John Masefield, copyright 1912 by John Masefield.

**This Paperback Library edition is published
by arrangement with William Morrow & Company, Inc.**

Paperback Library books are published by Paperback Library, Inc. Its trademark, consisting of the words "Paperback Library" accompanied by an open book, is registered in the United States Patent Office. **Paperback Library, Inc., 315 Park Avenue South, New York, N.Y. 10010.**

"I must go down to the seas again, to
    the lonely sea and the sky,
And all I ask is a tall ship and a star
    to steer her by."

                        . . . John Masefield
                            Sea-Fever

To the lads who sailed in the "CAN DO" ship

CONTENTS

CHAPTER 1

BATTLE OF THE ATLANTIC

Lots of other Generals and Admirals have lifted the iron curtain of official silence from closely guarded secrets of World War II; I feel it's about time for me to let loose on some. Ancient mariners occasionally have stories which they've got to tell, and a glittering eye is on *you* now. . . .

Serious students of military strategy who have digested the reports of Eisenhower, Halsey, and "Howlin' Mad" Smith, can afford to skip this yarn. Pentagon historians will quote nothing from this volume, and the National War College will make no revisions in its curriculum based on the incidents related herein.

The perpendicular pronoun will inevitably play a prominent part in this story, but I can't help that. I am the skipper in this saga, and the skipper is involved, for better or for worse to some extent, in everything that happens in his bailiwick. If what happens is good, the skipper has a perfect right to be smugly modest in accepting the credit. When what happens is bad, if he is worth his salt, he steps up and takes the rap, even though he had little control over the event in question. After all, the skipper is supposed to *have* control.

I'll start off with an inside story of the international intrigue and interservice feudin' that went on near the Arctic Circle up in Iceland, early in the war. I know there will be repercussions and denials. Frostbitten soldiers, sailors, and airmen will mush through the blizzard, come in stomping the snow off their fur-lined boots, and growl, "That ain't the way I heerd it." But they will have a twinkle in their weather-beaten eyes and no malice in their stout hearts.

To begin with, I got up to Iceland in a rather unusual manner. I was transferred up there by the Japanese. Just prior to our entry into World War II, I was in England "advising" the British on the construction of a large seaplane base at Loch Ryan, Scotland, and was slated to command this base when and if we got into the war. It was one of the choice jobs available at that time for a naval aviator of Commander's rank, and I was very well satisfied with my prospects.

Then the Japs butted in and messed things up. First they knocked us flat on our aft at Pearl Harbor. Our British naval friends sympathized smugly with us over this "most extraordinary incident," and heaved a great sigh of relief that we were finally in it with them. Then the *Prince of Wales* and the *Repulse* got sunk, shaking the limeys to the core and blotting out their complacency.

These two unfavorable developments swept a lot of well-laid plans into the ash can, including those for the future employment of one Commander Gallery. The third naval disaster struck immediately in the form of a dispatch from Washington ordering me to proceed to Reykjavik, Iceland, to command the U.S. Fleet Air Base there.

Iceland lies just below the Arctic Circle halfway between Greenland and England. It dominates the North Atlantic and will always be a prime strategic spot. It is ideally located for anti-submarine warfare operations and is the logical place from which to run convoys skirting the winter ice to Murmansk.

The American and British military forces were unwelcome guests up there during World War II. For a thousand years the Icelanders had sat out the wars of the world as neutrals. When we muscled in, we found a few of the people were actively pro-Allies, a few pro-Nazi; but the great majority took a dim view of anyone moving in on them. They simply "vanted to be *alone.*" They were also very narrow-minded about it when some of our sentries shot a few of their citizens who didn't understand that "Halt" mean "Nema Stadar."

While we built up our camp at the Reykjavik airdrome early in 1942, the Battle of the Atlantic mounted to a grim climax; England faced grave danger of being starved into surrender. Our job was to help beat the submarine wolf packs off the convoys hauling food and arms to England.

Doing this job we had to work closely with the R.A.F. and British Navy; in fact, for all practical purposes, we operated as an R.A.F. squadron.

Air Commodore Lloyd of the R.A.F. turned out to be a grand teammate. He and I saw eye to eye on every operational question, though at first we were inclined to be somewhat skeptical of each other. He told me after we became close friends that he had feared at first that anyone whose ancestry was so obviously Gaelic as mine would necessarily make things as difficult as possible for His Majesty's representatives.

I assured him that I had no such feeling and that I bore no ill will whatever toward the British. "In fact," I said, "I'm eternally grateful to your ancestors for persecuting my ancestors so that I was born in the U.S.A."

Through association with the Air Commodore I acquired a unique honorary title, the order of D.D.L.M. I am the only officer in any branch of the U.S. Military Services to be so honored. As a matter of fact, I created the title, and bestowed it on myself. It came about in the following manner.

Co-operating with the British on a common job, I naturally had frequent exchanges of official memoranda with the Air Commodore and the British Admiral. When you send a letter to a senior British officer you must put a long string of initials after his name: D.S.O., K.C.B., C.B.E., etc., indicating the orders and decorations which he holds. When I signed my name I had nothing to put behind my name except "Junior," and that made no impression whatever upon our gallant allies.

So after I got to know my correspondents pretty well, found that they were regular fellows and had twinkles in their eyes, I began putting D.D.L.M. after my signature, knowing full well that sooner or later they would ask me what it meant.

Sure enough, one morning I met the Air Commodore in R.A.F. headquarters, and after saying, "Good morning, Dan, old man," and discussing various matters, he said, "I say, old boy, what does that D.D.L.M. that you put after your name mean?"

"Why," I said, "That's the American equivalent of your K.C.B." Of course, K.C.B., Knight Commander of the Bath, is one of the biggest and best decorations that the British have. So the Air Commodore was duly impressed.

He said, "That's splendid. That's fine. I didn't know you Americans had any such thing."

I could see the wheels going round inside his head as he tried to puzzle out the meaning of the cryptic initials. Finally he gave up and asked, "Just what does it stand for?"

I said, "It means 'Dan Dan the Lavatory Man.'"

It was important to get on an informal and friendly basis with the R.A.F. because we had some delicate mutual problems to solve including the classic snafu of the command setup for Iceland. I had too many bosses. Practically everybody in Iceland had some sort of authority to issue orders to me, and whenever they happened to think of it they did.

Actually I came under five "commanding" officers simultaneously: two U.S. Admirals, one U.S. Army General, the R.A.F. Air Commodore, and the Royal Navy Admiral. The Gospel, according to St. Matthew, says, "No man can serve two masters," but I found that having five masters is all right; the command relationships get so complicated that nobody knows who is really boss. By exercising a little judicious stupidity you can get your bosses debating among each other as to who does what to whom; the situation gets so confused that they finally let you write your own ticket. That's what they did with me, and it was quite obvious that the best way to get on with the war was to join the R.A.F. So we took our orders from the

R.A.F., sent our action reports to the British Admiralty, drew our pay from the U.S. Navy, and sank submarines for the United Nations.

Theoretically this arrangement was completely cockeyed and unworkable. If any of the chairborne strategists in the Pentagon had found out about it they would have condemned it immediately. But working under this arrangement we set the pace for the U.S. Navy's anti-submarine campaign, and with a twelve-plane squadron amassed the highest record of any squadron in the Navy; *eight* officially confirmed U-boat kills.

Working with the R.A.F., we mothered the convoys passing three hundred to five hundred miles south of Iceland, and kept planes over all convoys within our range from dawn to dark. In the winter months we took off several hours before the crack of dawn and flew home through several hours of darkness.

Flying through stinking weather at night and in fog, when the low-lying clouds around your airdrome have centers of solid rock and your wings load up with ice, is bad for your blood pressure. To keep enthusiasm for this kind of flying at a proper level the skipper has to take his regular turn out over the convoy lanes, too. I often wondered on some of those long night hops whether there was any really worthwhile future in the racket.

Another convoy route passed to the north of Iceland. The survivors of that murderous run from Reykjavik to Murmansk and back (back only if you were lucky) are the unsung heroes of the war. Our planes escorted these convoys as far as we could, and often the Luftwaffe relieved us on the station at the end of our range. Thus the convoys had air cover all the way to Murmansk, but most of the way it was hostile. If the Luftwaffe and the German Navy had been able to co-operate effectively, nothing would have gotten through on that run. On the few occasions when the German Air Force and the submarines did succeed in working together, they slaughtered the convoys. Luckily for us, the Luftwaffe and the German Navy usually didn't speak to each other.

Even while the Germans made a shambles of the North Atlantic and the United States East Coast during the winter of 1942-43, they didn't like it around Iceland. They got in their dirty work on the convoys while outside the range of our planes. The trail of wreckage astern of the convoys ended where our air umbrella began.

There was no glamour in the work we were doing, and some of the crews flew for months without ever seeing a submarine. The fighter and bomber boys in Europe and the carriers in the Pacific held the spotlight, hogged the headlines, and collected baskets full of medals. Most of my lads got nothing for their efforts but the European Theatre Ribbon. We began referring to the Commendation Ribbon—most modest of all awards—as "The Atlantic Fleet Navy Cross." But our boys in Reykjavik did some of the most difficult, dangerous and important flying of the war. It really burned me up when I left Iceland and found out how the medal racket worked elsewhere.

You can see officers at any Washington cocktail party today who were chairborne throughout the war, but whose chests are covered with ribbons for every theatre in which our soldiers got killed. They "earned" these ribbons by passing through the various theatres on sightseeing junkets with high government officials. Even some of the combat awards have a strong odor of dead fish about them.

But don't let me get started on that subject; I could write a whole book about the prostitution of medals—if I had asbestos paper to write on. Maybe some day I will—after I retire!

Sometimes the convoys were so trigger-happy by the time they got near Iceland that you had to approach them with caution. One of our planes flew through a couple of hundred miles of soup on instruments to find a convoy from England, doing a beautiful job of locating it by radar. He made an instrument letdown, breaking out about 200 feet, right over the convoy. The convoy had been escorted part way over by the Luftwaffe so they had every gun manned and the instant our plane broke out they let him have it. In the time it takes to recognize a PBY and cease firing they had knocked out one engine, shot half the tail away and wounded three of the crew. Our plane zoomed up into the overcast again, struggled back to Iceland on one engine, and flopped in the surf. We fished all the boys out of the water and nursed the wounded back to duty again.

My boys didn't even get the Purple Heart out of that episode. The Purple Heart is for "wounds inflicted by the enemy," and the Board of Awards in Washington claimed that this convoy was *friendly,* even though the British Admiral readily conceded that its behavior had been "most disagreeable."

Though the war at sea was deadly, we had only one big air raid while I was in Iceland. On an Easter Sunday morning the sirens wailed their ominous warning, the fighters scrambled, and we rushed to our air defense stations. Word soon flashed over the command circuits from the Air Force H.Q.: "Estimate thirteen JU-88's crossing the coast headed for Reykjavik airdrome." For the next five minutes the radar warning net tracked the as yet unseen menace, keeping us constantly informed of developments.

We crouched outside my command post and scanned the eastern sky. Suddenly my orderly yelled, "Here they come!" pointing to a perfect V formation of tiny specks outlined against the blue.

This was it—our first real baptism of fire. I wondered if I would be very cool when the bombs started bursting, calmly steadying the nerves of my young sailors, or would I knock people down scrambling for shelter myself?

However, as the specks drew closer it became apparent that something was happening which wasn't in the script. Those JU-88's were all flapping their wings very briskly. On a radar scope a flock of ducks at one thousand feet looks the same as a squadron of bombers at ten thousand.

17

I rushed back to the office and dashed off an urgent memorandum to Colonel Ed Morris, my opposite member in the Air Force, requesting that his air intelligence section furnish the Navy with full technical details of this revolutionary development in bombardment aircraft. I also pointed out that there were only twelve ducks in the flock when they crossed the airdrome and inquired what had become of the other one.

In his reply the Colonel made a very silly, unmilitary, and totally impracticable suggestion as to what I could do with that missing duck if I found it.

A rather complicated question of military jurisdiction came up a little later when the Air Force shot down their first JU-88 which had come over to photograph the harbor. Of course, there was great excitement that morning when the fighter pilot who made the kill flashed word that two of the occupants had parachuted to safety halfway between Reykjavik and Keflavik. Everybody on the island turned out to compete for the distinction of capturing the first German prisoners to be taken by U.S. Forces in World War II.

Two Army Colonels enroute from Reykjavik to Keflavik in a jeep apprehended the fugitives and attempted to smuggle them out of the Reykjavik area and deliver them to their own general at Keflavik. However, a squad of M.P.'s from Reykjavik overhauled them and demanded the prisoners, because after all they had come down in the Reykjavik area. The Colonels indignantly refused to give them up and finally the M.P.'s had to surround and capture both the Colonels and the Nazis and haul them all back to the proper headquarters.

There was a lot of good-natured rivalry and mutual ribbing between our naval flyers and the Army Air Force. We burned up our brothers-in-arms by making the first landing on Meeks Field, their brand-new bomber base at Keflavik. This field was being built by Navy Seabees, so we worked out a deal involving a few cases of beer with the Navy civil engineer in charge of construction to let us know as soon as he got about two hundred yards of the first runway completed. We had a little utility plane over at our place which could get in and out of a much smaller field than any of the army planes, so as soon as our secret agent passed the word to us I climbed into this little bug, flew over and landed on the partly finished runway. This was regarded by the entire Air Force as a typical dirty, underhanded Navy trick.

Although there was plenty of this sort of horseplay and monkey business on the ground, we were playing for keeps out over the convoy lanes. After hunting submarines amid icebergs, sleet, and arctic gales our crews needed all the relaxation we could give them. The gym, enlisted men's recreation center, and officers' club, were popular and noisy places.

The movie hall was jammed every night. We only got about ten films a month from the States so a lot of the shows were repeaters, but the boys would pack the hall anyway. In some shady manner we acquired permanent title to one pretty good film called *Boom Town*. Whenever our regular shipment of films turned out to be a lot of tripe we would show *Boom Town* again. It played to standing-room-only audiences so often that eventually everybody knew the sound track by heart and the audience would raise the roof panting out the dialogue in the hot love scenes. We finally painted "Boom Town Theatre" over our marquee. It wasn't a bad picture—when there was nothing else to see.

Soon after the opening of the officers' club it seemed that perhaps we were having too much club life. We fumbled our first three opportunities to sink subs due to buck fever, bad luck, and inattention to seemingly minor details. I read the riot act to the boys and announced that our recently opened officers' club was hereby closed until we got our first kill. This was cruel and unusual punishment, but my platform was that I would much rather be a son of a bitch and help win the war, than to help lose it and be thought a swell guy.

During the era of the closed club Lieutenant Hopgood, enroute to meet a convoy coming up from England, caught the *U-464* surfaced about fifty miles from the convoy and crippled her so she couldn't submerge, but could still limp along on the surface. Hopgood expended all his depth charges on his first attack, and his single .30 caliber gun was useless against the sub's thick-skin and heavy AA battery. In the messy weather the sub soon shook off our circling plane by running into a fog bank. Meantime, a British destroyer left the convoy at full speed in answer to Hoppy's radio report of his attack. Hopgood flew toward the convoy until he found the speeding destroyer, advised her how to steer, and then flew back to hunt for the U-boat again. By this time the fog had lifted a bit and he found the sub, heading for an Icelandic fishing vessel a few miles away. As Hopgood circled, the sub went alongside the little trawler and the Nazis boarded the fishing vessel, abandoned and scuttled the U-boat, and laid a course toward Germany.

Hoppy duly reported all this by radio and spent the next couple of hours shuttling back and forth between the trawler and the oncoming destroyer, coaching the destroyer how to steer.

This was an exciting three hours in all the R.A.F. and Royal Navy operations rooms in England, as well as in ours up in Iceland. Hoppy's first electrifying messages telling that he had a cripple on his hands but couldn't finish it off had brought everybody in England to the operations rooms. For the rest of the morning Vice Admirals, Air Marshals and their staffs sat with their ears glued to the radio following the dramatic developments at sea.

Hoppy's radio reports right up to the final one had been masterpieces of correct official phraseology giving a terse, clear and complete picture of all the essential details of the changing action as it occurred. Finally he came through with the big punch line that we were waiting for: "Destroyer is alongside trawler and had taken off fifty-two prisoners." Then, shifting from code to plain English he continued, "Personal message for Commander Gallery: Sank Sub—open club!"

We opened the club all right. We damned near blew the roof off the joint. But Coastal Command Headquarters in London were a bit puzzled over that final message, and even after the Air Commodore, Iceland, explained it to them, they considered it "most extraordinary."

Another tale in connection with Hoppy's exploit is the legend of the "skipper's pants." With the big celebration and reopening of the club at its height, we conceived the happy idea of obtaining a suitable trophy of this victory to grace the lounge of the officers' club. Obviously the most suitable trophy would be the Nazi skipper's pants.

Next morning I addressed an official letter to the First Lord of the Admiralty in London, outlining briefly what had happened, explaining the American expression "caught with your pants down" and its obvious application to the previous day's work, and requesting that when the British destroyer arrived in England with the prisoners, the skipper's pants be forwarded to the Fleet Air Base. To make the deal legal, and to prevent leaving the German skipper in an embarrassing position, I sent a pair of my own khaki pants along with this letter, and forwarded the correspondence through the British Admiral in Iceland.

At first the idea of addressing the First Lord of the Admiralty with such an irregular proposal horrified the Admiral. But the Air Commodore persuaded him to "bung it on in" to London. By return mail I received a very pleasant letter from the First Lord assuring me that my request would be given due consideration.

A month or so later a very stuffy communication came in from the Director of Naval Intelligence, calling my attention to the Geneva Convention and its provisions prohibiting the humiliation of prisoners, etc., etc., and regretting that my request could not be granted.

I took a very dim view of the matter. I didn't mind the malarkey about the Geneva Convention anywhere near as much as I did the outrageous injustice of not even getting *my own pants back*.

All the time we were in Iceland the menacing shadow of a great ship hung over us. This ship was the *Tirpitz,* sister of the *Bismarck,* which broke through the Denmark Strait early in 1941, sank the *Hood,* and crippled the *Prince of Wales,* only sixty miles from Reykjavik. The one thing that stopped the *Bismarck* from ravaging the Atlantic convoy lanes was a lucky hit by an aircraft torpedo, which jammed her rudders, so that although otherwise undamaged, she circled helplessly until the home fleet closed in and hammered her to pieces.

I was obsessed with the idea that the *Tirpitz* might try the same thing. The unbelievable punishment which the *Bismarck* took before she sank indicated that torpedoes were the only weapon that could really hurt this class of ship. We had the only aerial torpedoes in Iceland, but our delivery vehicles were lumbering Catalina amphibians with a top speed of around 120 m.p.h.—they would be clay pigeons for the radar-controlled AA batteries of the *Tirpitz,* if we went in unsupported. The *Tirpitz* had the terrific advantage of choosing her own time to attempt the break-through, and I knew that with her high speed she could give the home fleet the slip, just as the *Bismarck* had done, any time she saw fit.

I knew that, if this happened, I would be awakened some night and handed a very simple message from Washington or London saying: *"Tirpitz* will pass through Denmark Strait just before daylight. Go get her!"

This recurring nightmare haunted me throughout the first six months in Iceland. If we had to tackle that job by ourselves it would have been a suicide mission. We had made up our minds that if this situation actually arose, we would give it the old college try, but we all knew the chance of getting even one of our torpedoes into the target would be extremely remote. The odds would be very long against any of us returning from that clambake.

However, I also believed that with proper support from

fighters and bombers we could put the *Tirpitz* on the bottom. But a co-ordinated attack of Army fighters, R.A.F. bombers, and U.S. Navy torpedo planes cannot be improvised on the spur of the moment. It requires careful planning and a lot of practice; and nobody in Iceland lost sleep over the *Tirpitz* except me.

"Why should the *Tirpitz* make a break?" they said. "Even if she gets loose, her days will be numbered and she will eventually be cornered and sunk. The Germans will never try it."

Hindsight shows they were right. However, I raised such a fuss that eventually they began to listen to me, and we organized an aerial task force and drew up a detailed plan for her destruction in case she tried to crash out as the *Bismarck* had done.

When I broached this plan to the British Admiral, Iceland, having finally sold it to the Air Force and R.A.F., his immediate reaction to it was: "You can't do that. The *Tirpitz* is Commander in Chief Home Fleet's bird!"

I finally convinced him that if Commander in Chief's "bird" ever got so far from home as Denmark Strait, it would become our painful duty to reluctantly let the bird have both barrels, and to hope that we could explain matters to C. in C.'s satisfaction after the *Tirpitz* was sunk.

The British Admiral, Iceland, at that time was Admiral Dalrymple-Hamilton, who commanded the *Rodney* at the kill of the *Bismarck*. After we had finally persuaded him, he rather liked our plan, particularly the detailed time schedule for the attack which we appended to it. This time schedule was very important, because the whole purpose of the plan was to tie up the *Tirpitz* AA batteries for the last three minutes that were absolutely vital to get our Catalinas into effective torpedo range. Several dozen events were programmed in this schedule, which included every move that the fighters, bombers, and torpedo planes were to make, from take-off to the knockout punch.

The final entries on the schedule were:

Zero minus 5 minutes: Fighters strafe decks and knock out AA batteries.

Zero hour: B-17's—deliver high-level attack.

Zero plus 3 minutes: Catalinas—launch torpedoes.

Zero plus 5 minutes: *Tirpitz* blows up and sinks.

The plan was submitted to London and Washington, they approved, and we held numerous dress rehearsals for it. Every time a British or U.S. battleship came to Iceland, we would have a *"Tirpitz* drill." I had a hell of a time persuading the Air Force fighters to venture out of sight of land on these rehearsals, even though a battleship had to be almost aground to be in sight of land in average Icelandic weather. But we eventually got our aerial team clicking like Lou Boudreau's pick-off play and I'll always regret that the *Tirpitz* didn't try to steal third.

After one of our *"Tirpitz* drills" Colonel Ed Morris, the Air Commodore, the British Admiral and I went out to the *King George V,* to discuss the operation with Commander in Chief, Home Fleet. It was a bitter day in the middle of January.

As we left the ship after our conference two British sailors took station at the foot of the gangway to help the brass into the Admiral's barge. When the boat shoved off, one of the sailors slipped on the icy platform and plunked into the near-freezing water. His buddy promptly hauled him back on the gangway again, and, although both were drenched with icy brine, they snapped to attention and stood at salute while the boatswain's mate finished piping the barge away.

I complimented Admiral Dalrymple-Hamilton on this "Good show . . . traditions of Nelson . . . and all that sort of thing."

"Nothing at all, old boy," the Admiral replied modestly, "I'm sure any of your sailors would have done the same thing."

"I suppose so," I said, but then every one of my Irish ancestors rose up in their graves and compelled me to add: "Except, of course, no American sailor would have fallen overboard in the first place."

The *Tirpitz* did come out once, on the Fourth of July, 1942. We ran the full gamut of emotions that day, from frantic alarm to delighted and confident anticipation; then amazed unbelief; and finally deep humiliation.

Early that morning we got a flash from the Admiralty in London, *"Tirpitz* sighted rounding North Cape."

It so happens that there are two North Capes. One is at the uppermost tip of Norway, and the other at the top of Iceland only sixty miles from Reykjavik. Although the Admiralty had guaranteed us at least twenty-four hours' warning of any attempted break-through, everybody jumped to the conclusion that it was *our* North Cape, and panic broke loose all over the airdrome to arm the planes and launch the attack before it was too late. However, it soon became clear that the dispatch referred to the North Cape in Norway.

That put a different aspect on the matter. The *Tirpitz* was heading into a booby trap! The high strategy boys in London were trying to slip one last convoy through on the murderous Murmansk run; that convoy was now approaching the North Cape of Norway. German planes and subs were giving it a terrific beating, but lurking about sixty miles astern of it was a naval task group with the U.S.S. *Washington* and the *King George V,* sent out for the specific purpose of polishing off the *Tirpitz* in case she went for the bait of the lightly escorted convoy.

As we watched this situation developing on the big chart in the operations room the Air Commodore remarked to me, "It looks like this is going to be the best Fourth of July since you blokes declared your independence."

About noon we intercepted the unbelievable message from London: "All warships retire to the west at high speed. Merchant vessels scatter and make best of way to Murmansk!" Too stunned and ashamed to say a word, we just drifted out of headquarters, went back to our huts, and wept or cursed.

Of course Pearl Harbor and Singapore were still fresh in the Admiralty's mind at that time. Many of our finest battleships had been sunk in the previous seven months, and the dockyards were jammed with badly damaged ships. The Admiralty was taking no chances on getting two more big ships out on a limb where the Luftwaffe might nail them. But I would rather not try to explain that to the merchant sailors who saw our big ships desert them.

When the *Washington* came into Reykjavik a few days later her people wouldn't come ashore. They didn't want to face their friends, although God knows all they did was to carry out orders which allowed them no discretion.

Until May, 1943, we were losing the Battle of the Atlantic. The grim toll of shipping sunk by submarines ran over half a million tons per month and England's plight was becoming desperate. During the winter of 1942-43 the only faint ray of hope was the fantastic shipbuilding program just getting into high gear in the United States. For a time we defeated the German submarines in our shipyards, while they ran amuck on the high seas in the areas which shore-based airplanes couldn't reach. We kept our heads above water by the ghastly expedient of launching ships almost as fast as the Nazis sank them.

In May, 1943, the tide of battle turned with dramatic suddenness. From that time on the avalanche of ships going down our building ways exceeded the sinkings by a constantly increasing margin. In addition, very long range land planes and small aircraft carriers finally extended our air umbrella to cover the whole North Atlantic and we broke the back of the U-boat fleet by making one hundred kills in May, June and July. The Nazis never recovered from that crippling slaughter. From that time on the once deadly submarine menace degenerated to a mere nuisance.

The German submarine designers worked frantically on snorkel and on new and revolutionary types of submarines. But they couldn't get them finished in time to be of any use. We sealed the fate of the Axis in those three months, off the shores of Newfoundland, Greenland, Iceland and England. We won the Battle of the Atlantic and paved the way for the large scale strategic bombing of Germany and the invasion of Normandy.

Twice within thirty years German submarines have had the Allies hanging over the ropes, on the verge of a knock-out; once in the winter of 1917 and again in 1941-42. New and more deadly types of submarines are in existence today. If we ever have to fight a third world war the Battle of the Atlantic will again be a crucial battle. All of us who were up in Iceland will say, "This is where we came in, we know the rest of this picture." I hope we don't have to lose several million tons of shipping to learn the same lessons all over again.

Anti-submarine warfare is a highly specialized business. It's a lot different from "wild blue yonder" flying, and you don't get a submarine hunting license when they pin a pair of wings on you at flying school. You have to fly many nautical miles over deep water where whales, porpoises, and "Mother Carey's chickens" live. You must know that those latitude and longitude lines which are so clear on the chart are very faint on the ocean, but they are there if you know how to find them. You have to rub elbows with ships, learn to speak their language, understand their habits, and have a seaman's eye for their silhouettes. You must at least know that the sharp and blunt ends of a "boat" are respectively the ship's bow and stern.

The obvious moral to the above is that to insure that our country's beaches will never again be strewn with wreckage and soaked with oil as they were in 1942, we must keep a strong naval air arm. But if I get going on this, we'll be up for the whole arctic night, and won't get to bed until the sun comes up next April. So let's take a look at the lighter side of life in the land of the midnight sun.

CHAPTER 2

SNAFU IN THE ARCTIC

When I had arrived in Reykjavik late in December, 1941, I had found the situation grim. For six months our Navy flyers had eked out a miserable existence, knee-deep in mud, waiting for their ship to come in. All that came in was me!

Our boys had taken refuge in dilapidated Nissen huts, abandoned by the British, through which the arctic winds howled with glee. The well-dressed young man about camp wore long flannel drawers, and at night without our eiderdown sleeping bags the boys would have frozen.

The galley was equipped with salvaged junk; the food was terrible. The principal plumbing necessities were of the Chic Sale variety, and you couldn't take a bath even if you wanted to. While struggling to stay alive under these conditions we had the little problem of guarding the North Atlantic convoy lanes in the worst weather in the world.

My first job obviously was to keep the planes flying and help get the convoys through; next, to get decent living conditions established. I thought that my biggest problem was going to be how to keep the boys from blowing their tops after a few months in that godforsaken hole.

It seemed as if the top brass in Washington had forgotten us. But soon our long-awaited ship came in, and discharged one naval air base complete with spare parts; we lost no time in setting it up. *Everybody* pitched in to get the new camp built. One day I caught the doctor, the paymaster and the chaplain blasting rocks out of the frozen ground with dynamite to build a machine gun emplacement in a slit trench they were digging. From that day forward I knew the United States couldn't lose! This was really "total" war.

Our Quonset huts went up fast. There is nothing luxurious about a Quonset hut, but it does provide adequate shelter, even in Iceland, and our planners back in Washington sent us a lot more than the bare walls and frames. Every hut had electric lights, kerosene stove, automatic phonograph, and radio.

We made our own electricity with Diesel generators which had to be kept running at constant speed, because some of our equipment around the camp wouldn't work right if the voltage or frequency varied. At first the boys who stood watch in the generator hut suspected me of being either a mind reader or a magician, because I often called them up from my hut to bawl them out for running the generators a little bit too fast or too slow. Sometimes the machines differed so little from the correct speed that you couldn't tell it by looking at the lights, but the dials on the control panel always showed that my beef was justified. The secret was my radio-victrola and an album of records by Toscanini. When the music sounded like Toscanini I knew the generators were exactly on the right speed. When it came out sour, I knew it wasn't Toscanini who was off the beam.

The occupants of each hut used their own ingenuity in arranging their fourteen bunks, lockers and furniture. Each hut had room in the front for a card and checker table near the stove, writing desks off to the side, and a radio near the door. As time went by, easy chairs, made out of discarded shipping crates, homemade lamp shades and rugs began to appear. One hut even had a make-believe grandfather's clock standing by the stove. Of course, every square inch of wall and locker space was inevitably plastered with lurid reminders, clipped from *Esquire,* of the one big comfort of home which was missing.

Complaints about the lack of home cooking soon stopped. I wish you could have seen the galley equipment that was set up there—excellent ranges, ovens and steam kettles, automatic dishwashers and driers, Deep-Freeze lockers, and fine butcher shop equipment. When I brought the British Air Commodore over to inspect it his eyes bulged out like a tromped-on toad. He went away muttering to himself about the hardships the poor colonials have to put up with!

After the ovens in our galleys began roasting, we received daily tribute to the excellent work of our cooks. Every day at noon and every evening at suppertime a dozen or so British and U.S. Army truck drivers would find some excuse for stopping at Fleet Air Base and "bumming a meal off of us." I never objected, because as long as all those vehicles lined up on our main street at chow time, I knew without going any further that our cooks were doing all right.

For the first couple of months after we got our new camp built, rats overran the place. Our good Navy chow attracted visitors from all over Iceland. Although we welcome our hungry brothers-in-arms in the Air Force and the Army, and our allies in the R.A.F. and British Navy, we had to draw a line someplace. We put a bounty of a dollar per head on rats. Catching and shooting rodents became a profitable as well as exciting pastime. Large bounties were collected at first, and after a couple of weeks I saw no more rats nosing around our streets. Our "game warden's" office, however, continued to do a brisk business, and it took me several weeks to find out that I was paying bounties on rats killed in every camp in Iceland. My boys paid two bits apiece to their friends in the adjacent R.A.F., Norwegian, and U.S. Army camps for dead rats, and smuggled them into our place to collect a nice profit. However, our soda fountain made money for the welfare fund so fast that we decided to ignore the rat racket. By cleaning out the surrounding camps we were helping ourselves anyway.

During the long arctic nights we held grave round-table discussions about a name for our camp. The one we finally evolved had an Icelandic or Eskimo air about it, but on closer inspection contained some good plain American advice to all hands. It was "Kwitcherbellyakin."

We actually had very few squawks, but many of us thought the Gregorian calendar with its seven-day week was much too complicated for the unvarying routine which we soon fell into. One day was just about the same as another up there. You had a certain number of operational flights to make; everybody had to get three square meals; and you had to do something to keep the boys amused in the off hours. Revising our calendar, we adopted a "week" having only three days—Yesterday, Today and Tomorrow. We detailed one yeoman to keep track of the real date in case an unforseen emergency arose which required writing an official letter to Washington.

One thing that our logistic planners back home omitted from their calculations was the need for a recreation hall and gymnasium during the long arctic nights. They sent us plenty of recreational gear, but no place to use it. We remedied this oversight by "misappropriating" two of the supply officer's big storehouses to this purpose. I figured that, if necessary, I would rather explain why we left some of our equipment out in the weather to spoil, than to have to explain why the boys were going nuts. Admiral King put a terse O.K. on that decision when he stopped in at our place some months later on his way home from a conference in London.

The arrival of our first shipment of recreational equipment from the United States brought about an incident which helped us to by-pass protocol, break the ice, and get acquainted with the British.

Opening up the boxes in this consignment like a bunch of kids on Christmas morning, we found, among other things, a pushball, which we promptly blew up to its full five-foot diameter. Exploring the boxes for more loot, we left the pushball sitting outside the gymnasium unattended.

You should never leave anything as big and light as a

pushball unattended in Iceland, because the wind comes along and blows it away. This happened to our pushball. I came out of the gym just in time to watch it bounce down the hill, over the bluff, and into the water. It sailed rapidly across the inlet and grounded on the opposite shore where a British antiaircraft battery had its camp.

I wanted that pushball back, so I picked up my field telephone to call the Commanding Officer of the antiaircraft battery and ask his help. Strange things often happened on our field telephone system, which consisted of a labyrinth of wires laid out on the ground. Very often connections got crossed, as they did this time.

I heard my friend across the way calling British Admiralty Headquarters and reporting: "The biggest bloody mine you've ever seen in your life has just washed ashore at our camp, and will you please send a bomb disposal party over to deal with it."

I hung up without saying a word. A few minutes later I called Admiralty Headquarters and reported that we too had seen this mine wash ashore, that we had a qualified bomb disposal squad, and that if the Admiralty wished us to do so, we would be glad to deal with this situation.

Of course, there was nothing in the world that the Admiralty wished more at that time than to have somebody else take this nasty job off their hands. They promptly replied that this would be "quite satisfactory."

So, I rushed around to the adjoining huts, rounded up about a dozen helpers, explaining the pitch to them, and we organized a bomb disposal squad on the spot. We had all read enough about bomb disposal to have a pretty good idea as to what equipment we needed and how to go through the proper motions. We commandeered a half a dozen rifles, scrambled around the camp and grabbed a portable field telephone set, a couple of voltmeters, a stethoscope, and some small tool boxes. Dumping this equipment into jeeps, we roared over to the British camp, where we found a crowd of our allies all standing back at a respectful distance, casting nervous glances at the "mine."

The arrival of our business-like group of American experts obviously relieved the tension. We immediately stationed our sentries and pushed the crowd back to a safer distance. Leading out our field telephones we placed one of them at the "mine" and the other about a hundred yards back, so that the mine disposal boys could phone back every move they made to be recorded in a notebook for the guidance of future mine disposal squads, in case they made the wrong move and blew themselves up.

After a few minutes of hocus-pocus with the stethoscope and voltmeters and much telephoning back and forth, we finally gave the signal that the big moment was at hand. As the crowd watched in awed silence we unscrewed the valve, let the air out, and got the hell out of that camp as fast as we could.

Concurrently with this international leg-pulling the camp construction moved along, the Seabees performing their usual miracles. The last thing to go up was the officers' club and mess. By this time we proudly exhibited our place to sightseers. Showing some Army nurses around the camp, one of our boys gloatingly pointed out what we had already done and described future plans. Having seen our ultramodern galley and well-equipped recreation hall and gymnasium, the gals were about ready to believe *anything* was possible for the Navy. Going through the nearly-finished officers' club my gallant young gentleman pointed out the window at the forbidding rocky beach in front and said, "The next convoy is bringing us a shipload of white sand from Miami, and we'll have a regular beach out there by summer." The nurses believed this story implicitly and it spread through all the Army camps on the island, causing great indignation and a few threats to write to Congressmen.

Even though we never got our beach, we did have some almost equally improbable things. Our proudest possession was a pair of palm trees near the main entrance to the camp.

Trees do not grow in Iceland. So when the leading chief from our metalsmith shop came into my office one day and said, "Captain, we ought to have some palm trees around this place," I thought to myself: *Now it begins— here's the first one we have to ship home in a straitjacket.*

However, I humored him and listened to his proposal. When he got through outlining his plan I quoted Joyce Kilmer: "Only God can make a tree."

The Chief replied, "Yeah, we know that, Cap'n, but we'd like to have a shot at it, anyway."

Within a week two authentic looking palm trees had grown on our main street. The "trunks" were steel pipes about six inches in diameter which we wrapped with burlap to give them a tapering and rough appearance. The "stems" of the leaves were reinforcing rods for concrete runways, bent to the proper curvature, and we cut the "leaves" from sheets of tin obtained by flattening out five-gallon kerosene cans. A coat of green paint plus some worn-out softballs for coconuts completed the simulated tropical job.

These trees got to be quite famous, and it eventually became routine when plush four-engine planes had to stop for gas in Iceland enroute from Washington to London, or vice versa, for all the "VIP's" to come over to our place and have their pictures taken under the palm trees in Iceland. Even Admiral King relaxed and grinned during his inspection of the place when he came to this horticultural miracle.

More monkey business by our versatile metalsmiths provided us with conspicuous fire hydrants on every street corner and in front of every hut in the camp. Casual visitors must have figured that we had overdone things a bit on fire protection. However, the hydrants were all phonies, manufactured from our great oversupply of one-hundred-pound water-fillable practice bombs. In their spare time the metalsmiths welded two short lengths of pipe on the side of each bomb to simulate hose connections, stuck a large nut on top, painted everything a brilliant red, and planted them around all over the camp with the tail fins buried in the ground. The result was a perfect facsimile of a fire plug, and the camp was a puppy dog's paradise.

Just between you and me, it wasn't nearly as cold in Iceland as we like to make out that it was. The Gulf Stream goes close by the South Coast and makes the winter climate there milder than it is in New England. There are no Eskimos, and the only polar bear ever seen there in the memory of the oldest inhabitants drifted in from the North on an ice floe during an unusually severe winter twenty years ago. During the two winters that I spent there we didn't have more than about three weeks of ice skating on the Reykjavik pond.

But of course that wasn't the story we told about the weather in our letters home. We figured that if there was any bragging to be done about the climate we would let the Reykjavik Chamber of Commerce do it. Everybody at home visualized Iceland as a land buried in snow and ice where the people lived in igloos, and we let them keep on thinking so. Every time we had a moderate New England snowstorm, which wasn't often, we hustled our photographers out to take pictures of the deepest drifts for the edification of the folks back home—and of the Navy Department.

We didn't do this just for the fun of it; we had a far-reaching motive. Some of the requisitions that we sent to Washington for furniture, special clothing, and recreational equipment were a bit on the Park Avenue side. When the supply people back in Washington got requisitions for overstuffed sofas, pianos, and bowling alleys they would say, "What screwball submitted that pipe dream?" and get ready to reply with a "Don't-you-know-there's-a-war-on" letter. But when they looked at the bottom of the form and saw that it came from Reykjavik, Iceland, they would usually say, "Well, for those poor

35

guys up there we will approve this." We like to call ourselves the F.B.I.'s, meaning, "Forgotten Bastards of Iceland," but, as a matter of fact, we were far from forgotten.
We were well taken care of.

In practicing this deception about the climate we were
following a precedent that goes back to the time when
Iceland and Greenland were named by the Norsemen.
Most of Greenland is buried under an ice cap thousands
of feet thick. Back in 800 A.D. the Vikings, who settled in
Iceland and liked the place, deliberately hung these misleading names on the two islands to discourage immi-
grants from flocking up to Iceland and crowding them.

As the standard of living and recreational facilities of
our camp improved, the neighbors began moving in on
us, just as the Vikings had feared would happen to them.
Our well-stocked ship's store became so popular that we
had to put a limit on individual purchases to shop hoard-
ing and the black market operations. This led to a minor
rhubarb with the U.S. Army in which I got myself into
the deplorable position of deliberately obstructing military justice.

One day about noon I met a soldier headed down the
main street of our camp, toward the gate, his arms piled
so high with cartons of cigarettes, tubes of shaving cream,
and boxes of chocolate bars that he could hardly walk. As
I passed him I remarked, "That's quite a load you've got
there, soldier." Without batting an eye, this brave young
G.I. replied, "Yessir, it's all I can carry *this trip,*" and
wended his way slowly down to the gate and out of the
camp.

Then I got to thinking, "I wonder how come a soldier
can buy all that stuff in our store when we have just rationed sales to our own people?" I sent for the paymaster
and asked him to look into it.

The paymaster burst back into my office a few minutes
later in a state of amazed indignation and reported that
his store had been robbed! My soldier friend had simply
hung around until the store closed for lunch, and while

all hands were stuffing themselves had jimmied the padlock on the Quonset hut and boldly helped himself.

It took only a few minutes checking by my Gestapo to locate the culprit at an adjoining Army camp. When it turned out that he was the Commanding Officer's orderly, I gleefully wrote an official letter requesting that hereafter the Commanding Officer obtain his personal supplies through official channels rather than by taking such irregular short cuts.

However, when they tried to call me as a witness at the soldier's subsequent court-martial I refused to answer the summons, and sent back word that, in my opinion, any combat infantryman with that much initiative, nerve and guts should be promoted to sergeant instead of court-martialed.

Another larceny committed at our camp some months later nearly caused me to blow a gasket and became quite a "cause célèbre" in Iceland. Our Marines had established what we thought was an airtight sentry system around the camp, so not even a rat could slip in without their knowing it. I had boasted to all the surrounding camp commanders about how good our sentries were, and many of my friends had actually found by experience that if they didn't have proper credentials they couldn't get in or out of the camp, scrambled eggs or no scrambled eggs.

Then some arctic Jesse James absconded with the big bass fiddle from our camp orchestra! When the word went round that the bass fiddle had been stolen from the Fleet Air Base right from under the noses of the vigilant Leathernecks, raucous raspberries resounded all around Reykjavik.

It turned out to be an inside job. That "doghouse" was flown out of Iceland in the gun blister of one of our own PBY's when we sent a squadron to participate in the North African Invasion. A year later when I had command of an escort carrier task group in the Atlantic we stopped in at Casablanca for a couple of days and I made a special trip up to Port Lyautey, where our PBY's were based, to say hello to my old shipmates from Iceland and also to make discreet inquiries about that fiddle. Sure enough—it was there! We put the finger on the sailor who had committed the burglary. I confronted and denounced him, and received a full confession of his guilt. The obvious moral was that the arm of the law is long, can reach all the way from the Arctic to the Tropics, and we let it go at that.

However, getting back to Iceland at the time of the robbery, the Marine Major really put the blast on his sentries during the uproar about the fiddle. While the heat was on I played about the dirtiest trick you can play on the Marines; I swiped three of their rifles.

It is, of course, a great point of pride with the Corps that a marine and his rifle are inseparable. It would require at least five husky soldiers and a couple of small sailors to take a marine's rifle away by force. One night just before the movies, after the sentry watches had been relieved, I saw three off-duty marines park their rifles in the storm entrance to the recreation hall and go inside to see the show. My orderly was off on some errand; everybody else was inside the hall; so it was a simple matter for me to grab the guns and hotfoot it back to my hut without being seen by anyone.

For the next three days the harried expression on the faces of our usually cocky Marines indicated that all was not well.

Finally I sent for the Major and presented him with the guns. He told me afterwards that they had ransacked every building in the camp—except my hut—searching for those rifles. He also claimed that he was just on the point of reporting the loss to me when I gave them back, and would have done it much sooner except that he was so sure they couldn't possibly have gotten out of the camp, etc. etc.

I hope you won't think from anything I have said that I mean to belittle the Marines. The Marines are the finest fighting outfit in the world today and I am proud that they are a part of the Navy. But I don't mind tagging them out if I happen to catch them off base.

Of course, when you come down to brass tacks the job of the Marine Corps is very simple. The Navy transports them to some place where there is a suitable landing beach and the inhabitants are hostile. The ships then hold a sort of a Chinese New Year's celebration, tossing a lot of high explosives ashore and making a hell of a racket. As soon as all the palm trees and native huts have been blown up, the Marines go ashore and take possession of the beach head. After that all they've got to do is to advance about ten miles inland and start building Quonset huts for the Army, who will show up as soon as the situation is well in hand.

The official opening of our recreation hall was a gala event to which we invited all the top brass in Iceland. There were three Army hospitals with *nurses* in Iceland, and it was obviously my duty as Commanding Officer to stand in well with the chief nurses, so that they would be favorably inclined toward allowing the younger nurses to date my boys from the Fleet Air Base. Complying with this obligation, I invited the three chief nurses to the grand opening, sent my car to pick them up, and instructed my driver to stand by at the O.O.D.'s shack to take the ladies home after the show.

When the premiere was over, all the official guests, including the nurses, adjourned to my hut for coffee, sandwiches, and "one for the road." At this gathering one of the Generals graciously offered to take the nurses home. In the midst of all the social activity I forgot to pass this word to my driver. So after speeding the last departing guest into the night, I crawled into my sack and slept soundly until six o'clock the next morning.

On the way to breakfast I stopped in at the O.O.D.'s shack and there sat my driver, heavy-eyed and sleepy, but with an accusing smirk on his sassy face. He was carrying out my orders and waiting to take the three chief nurses home!

He had spent an all-night vigil in a place where everybody who happened to be up and around in the camp would see him and wonder what he was doing. Every four hours during the night a new duty section of about thirty men mustered in the O.O.D.'s office before relieving the watch. Naturally they all recognized the Captain's driver and wanted to know why he was up so late. All night long he spread the happy word, "I'm waiting to take the Cap'n's gal friends home——he's got three of 'em down in his hut."

There was a marked increase in the deference with which I was treated by all hands from then on.

This saga of the three chief nurses, together with the fact that as related in the previous chapter I was one of the few officers in Iceland to lose a pair of pants while on duty there, caused exaggerated tales to circulate among the officers' messes on the island. I defended myself against these slanderous canards by pointing out that it is impossible to be a Don Juan in the Arctic, because in the summertime it is daylight all night long and in the winter you leave tracks.

Our gymnasium, in the "misappropriated" storehouse, was a godsend to the whole island. It housed the only good basketball court in Iceland; we made it available to all the nearby Army camps. Throughout the long winter nights the court was in constant use from 3:00 to 10:00 P.M. Some big league basketball was played in that gym, and the final series for the championship of Iceland, fought out between our boys and an Army tank company, aroused as much excitement and enthusiasm as any Army-Navy game back home. Thanks to a little soldier by the name of Fritch, who sank shots which I still say were impossible, they nosed us out.

Through a basketball game with the Army, one of America's fundamental war aims was impressed upon me in a diplomatic but pointed manner. At this game I noticed that a group of my own lads were rooting *against* our team. There was a lot of inter-hut rivalry involved

40

and a difference of opinion had developed as to who should be playing on our team.

We were beaten by a garrison finish, and at the end of the game, smarting from the ribbing of various Army officers, I gruffly informed the ringleader of our subversive rooters that if he and his mob didn't want to root for *our* team, they could stay away from the gym and make room for properly patriotic citizens who did.

Next morning I found a copy of the *Saturday Evening Post* laid out on my office desk opened to a double page spread advertising war bonds. The illustration featured a close-up of the grandstand at a baseball game with the fans expressing obvious and noisy disapproval of something happening down on the field. In big letters across the top of the page was the legend, "We are fighting for the right to boo the Dodgers!" Properly squelched, I said no more about that subject.

With the approach of summer, softball replaced basketball as the major sport. We had a league with ten teams in which the Marines managed to nose out my officers' team for the championship both seasons while I was up there. I played third base on the officers' team; and the sailor and marine umpires took great delight in calling all the close ones against me, just to hear me squawk, and to be able to say, very, very respectfully, of course, "Cap'n, sir, if you don't shut up, I'll have to heave you out of the game, sir."

During the summer months it was broad daylight throughout the night. This continuous daylight led to one of the Navy's greatest victories of the war over the Army Air Force. It was only a softball game, but it struck a great blow for freedom from a naval viewpoint.

Our Officers' softball team was pretty hot, and Colonel Ed Morris of the Army Air Force claimed that his was, too. We challenged his team several times but got no answer. So we began a needling campaign which reached its climax at an official luncheon given for Molotov and his naval aide, Admiral Guitcheraa Soffamy, when they passed through Iceland on the way to the United States. Morris and I sat next to each other, and from soup to nuts, I gave him a verbal hotfoot about the evasive tactics of his team. Morris went back to his headquarters with a high temperature, sent for his aide and said, "Write a letter to those goddam sailors accepting their challenge, and saying we will pin their ears back."

About six that evening I received the letter couched in flamboyant language, full of "whereases" and "now therefores," concluding with the statement, "We will play your team on any diamond in Iceland at any time after 0400 tomorrow morning." The Colonel, of course, expected us to reply in due time saying that we would play two weeks from next Saturday at 4:00 P.M., or something along those lines.

At dinner that evening I got my ball team together and said, "How about it, boys? 0400 tomorrow morning?" We all knew that the Air Force was having a big binge that night to celebrate knocking down their first Nazi photo plane a few days previously, and so this plan was judged to have extraordinary merit. We all turned in early for a good night's sleep, and our reply went back by officer messenger and was delivered to the Colonel in person, around eleven-thirty that night. By this time festivities at the Air Force camp were in full swing, and all the intrepid birdmen had a good head of steam up.

A bleary-eyed bunch of Army aviators showed up at 0400 the next morning. We set them down with one scratch hit and shut them out 13 to 0.

However, I wasn't always able to come out ahead of the Colonel. He was, of course, senior to me by one rank, and whenever I became too obnoxious he would remind me of this fact. In October, 1942, I made a flying trip to Washington for two days and while there was notified that I had been promoted to Captain. I lost no time in getting a uniform with four broad gold stripes on it, and as soon as I landed back in Reykjavik I made a beeline for Colonel Ed's H.Q., intending to blow him a loud

Bronx cheer and thumb my nose at him. I was due for my greatest disappointment of the war. There sat Morris as smug as a cat full of canaries au gratin, with Brigadier General's stars on his shoulders!

The midnight sun was responsible for the birth of a new international signal flag designed by the U.S.S. *Barnegat,* a seaplane tender attached to our base. It was a square black flag with a crescent moon and three white stars.

The *Barnegat* presented one of these flags to us which we hung in the lounge of our officers' club with an explanatory placard supplied by the *Barnegat.* The placard read as follows:

This is the Do-Not-Disturb-Flag. It was originated by the *Barnegat* in Iceland, where during the summertime it is daylight all night long. When the midnight sun is shining this flag is flown at the starboard main yardarm, after taps, to indicate to the people at the Fleet Air Base, who don't know any better, that it is time to go to bed and that the crew of the *Barnegat* are all in their bunks asleep.

To the *Barnegat's* outraged indignation, we added the following to their placard:

Note: During working hours no special flag is flown by the *Barnegat* to indicate the above condition.

For the first year that I was in Iceland the gentlemen's room in my hut was a rather primitive affair of modified Chic Sale type. The only reason why it should be tolerated at all *inside* the hut was that it had a chemical tank which, according to the manufacturer, was supposed to overcome the obvious objections to such an intimate arrangement and, you might say, to clarify the atmosphere.

Our logistic planners back home eventually thought of everything and at last one of our Seabees came around to my hut lugging a beautiful streamlined flushing job under his arm.

"I think you'll like this one better, Cap'n," he said, as he got busy ripping out the Chic Sale and hooking the new equipment into the camp's drainage system.

He was right. I liked it so much better that I decided the Spartan interior decoration scheme of a Quonset hut was out of keeping with this reminder of The American Standard of Civilized Life. So, aided by enthusiastic suggestions from practically all hands in the camp, I set out to create a suitable environment for it.

First we erected an ornate canopy over it, trimmed with ermine (obtained from a roll of cotton batting provided by the pharmacist's mates). We shopped all over Reykjavik to get suitable curtains for draping from the canopy. The whole camp aided in designing the great heraldic insignia which went up on the bulkhead behind the throne. We installed rose-colored indirect lighting suitable for encouraging the contemplative mood. A cushioned footrest, ash trays, and book shelves were all conveniently placed.

By the time we got through it was fit for a king—and looked as if it had been built for one to reign on.

However, we didn't want the users of this luxurious facility to forget there was a war on. So we installed a battery of field telephones within easy reach of the occupant of the throne. One was labeled, "Direct line to White House," another, "Number 10 Downing Street." On hooks adjacent to them hung a pair of relief tubes from PBY airplanes. One was labeled "Wilhelmstrasse," the other "Tokyo."

The final touch was a spare porcelain seat which we sawed in two. One half, embellished with the proverbial fur lining, was attached to the bulkhead where it would be the first thing seen by anyone entering the throne room. A placard below it said: "For use by my half-fast friends."

When the job was completed it became one of the

show places of Iceland, and my johnny was warmed by the fannies of many Very Important Persons in the Army, Navy and Air Force of Great Britain and the United States.

All these things happened during the midnight sun of 1942. Our camp by then was a thriving community with gravel streets, comfortable living quarters and plenty of recreational facilities.

At the beginning of this chapter I said my principal early worry had been how I was going to keep the boys from blowing their tops after the first six months. Six months had gone by and I was then sending for any of the lads who got off the beam, shaking my finger at them and saying, "Son, if you don't knock that off, I'm going to send you home."

By this time we were throwing our weight around daily over the convoys several hundred miles to the south of Reykjavik and were making life miserable for the German subs.

While we fought the Battle of the Atlantic up there near the Arctic Circle, our Pacific Fleet struggled back to its feet after Pearl Harbor, cleared its head, and started punching. We got radio accounts from the B.B.C. in London of the battles of Coral Sea, Midway, and Guadalcanal. By this time we were getting U.S. newspapers only a day or two after they were printed, and we gathered around in groups to read these papers as they came in. Of course they told us only what the Navy Department thought it was safe for the general public to know.

As each new convoy arrived it brought us confidential action reports from the Navy Department on battles fought several months previously. From these we got the real low-down on what was happening. We found out why we lost the *Lexington, Wasp, Hornet,* and *Yorktown;* how we got the four Jap carriers at Midway; how these desperate struggles in the dark were fought in Ironbottom Bay around Guadalcanal. . . . We pored over every word in these reports and envied our friends who were making history in the Pacific.

The more I read the more restless I got. This job in Iceland was vitally important, of course—and if we lost the Battle of the Atlantic we would lose the war. But I had spent twenty years of my life learning to be a naval officer and to fly airplanes from ships. I didn't want to sit out the greatest war in history on the beach. I wanted a ship.

In May, 1943, my prayers were answered. I got my orders to report to the United States to take command of an escort carrier.

I left Iceland with no regrets, and I still look back on it that way. It was rugged duty but we pulled our weight in the boat.

CHAPTER 3

A STAR TO STEER HER BY

Then I went down to sea in a ship—a simple, frail, and homely little baby flattop of 11,000 tons. Among the battleships, cruisers and the great ladies of the Essex class carriers, she seemed a Cinderella. But she was handy, happy-go-lucky, and didn't know the meaning of the word "impossible." Like Kipling's Aggie De Castrer. "She showed me the way to promotion and pay."

I won't say that I learned about women from her, but I did learn one thing: when you hitch your wagon to a star the sky is the limit to your cruising radius.

If your wagon is a ship, of course, you've got to have a good crew and you've got to be lucky. But with your towline secured to stellar cleats your crew *will* be good, and Lady Luck will be a "plank owner." I'm just a seafaring man but I think maybe this sailing direction also applies inside the six-fathom curve to life ashore.

When they broke the bottle over my ship's stem as she slid down the building ways on June 5, 1943, they gave her a name that made her plates twice as strong as the designer's slide rules said they were. It put extra power in her engines to take her wherever she had to go, and it entitled her to go places where bigger and sturdier ships could not prudently venture. They called her the *Guadalcanal*.

Astronomers may say that I'm mixing my metaphors, but the name was our star. On a little island in the South Pacific the Marines made it a star of the first magnitude. We who took that name to sea dedicated ourselves to living up to it, knowing full well that we had a big job cut out for us.

The *Guadalcanal,* CVE-60, was one of the fifty prefab-ricated, mass-produced jeep carriers turned out by assem-bly-line methods at the Kaiser Yard in Vancouver, Washington. The decision to build these ships caused the biggest argument in naval circles since Noah built the Ark. Every salt-water sailor and naval architect in the country shook his head in dismay. By pre-war Navy standards, these ships simply didn't make sense, and any-one with even a few years' seagoing experience could tell from a glance at the plans that no good would ever come of them.

A lot of people said so in no uncertain terms, too. When my crew was being formed I found it necessary to as-semble them and scotch some of the rumors that began to circulate around the waterfront.

One was to the effect that the ships were structurally unsound and would break in two in a seaway. I must admit this didn't seem too implausible at the time, espe-cially when you looked around the building yards and saw the farmers, shoe clerks, and high-school gals who were assembling the ships.

Strange things must have gone on during the night shifts in the Kaiser Yard when Rosie the Riveter was build-ing aircraft carriers. One day, shortly after we went in commission, Earl Trosino, my chief engineer, came up to the cabin gingerly holding a pair of pink silk panties by one corner. He had fished them out of the starboard main condenser. By sundown that day every man in our crew had his own theory as to how this bit of feminine 'twixt-wind-and-water rigging had gotten into our machinery. All explanations were much too ribald to be printed here.

That fantastic shipbuilding operation in the Kaiser Yard was typical of the way the industrial might and know-how of this country mobilized to win the war for us. Naval architecture is an ancient and intricate art, and all the shipbuilding trades are exclusive guilds, usually requiring a long apprenticeship. But on the banks of the Columbia River a vast shipyard with eleven building ways sprang up from a swamp overnight. People who didn't know the bow from the stern of a ship came from the inland states to build aircraft carriers in it. All over the country factories accustomed to building bridges, oil tanks, and farm machinery, built miscellaneous sections of ships. These sections poured into Vancouver by rail and were put on an assembly line as if they were automobile parts. Great chunks of ships were welded together in out-of-the-way parts of the yard, were picked up by huge cranes, carted down to the building ways, and hoisted into place.

Ships are usually built on the stocks rivet by rivet and plate by plate; but not in this mass production operation. I attended the launching of one ship on a Saturday. On the following Monday morning I saw the entire bottom of another ship, welded together clear out to the turn of the bilge, on that same building way. This was an assembly job rather than a conventional shipbuilding operation.

A bunch of amateurs, setting up assembly-line production for any kind of a ship, are taking a long chance. To do it for a specialized type like an aircraft carrier seems like a miscalculated risk. But the fifty-five jerry-built ships that crowded down those building ways in Vancouver performed at sea like professional men-of-war, and wrote several brilliant pages in American naval history.

If the Nazis and Japs could have seen that yard when it was going full-blast in 1943 I think they might have given up then and there. Generals and Admirals are prone now to expand on the brilliant military strategy that won the war for us. What really won it was the avalanche of war production that poured out of places like the Kaiser Yard, Ford's River Rouge Plant, and others like them all over the country. You can make some gawd-awful strategic bloopers and get away with it when you've got production like that to fall back on.

The strategists in the Navy Department all said "No" when Kaiser first came to Washington with his plans for the "jeep" carriers. But Kaiser got F.D.R.'s ear—we were losing the war at that time—and so he built them anyway.

I still don't believe some of the things which I know these ships actually did. . . . But of course the *Guadalcanal* could do anything.

While the ship moved toward the end of the production line, our crew assembled. As the new men reported from the cities, small towns and cornfields of the country, we handed each of them the following memo:

1. The motto of the *Guadalcanal* will be "Can Do," meaning that we will take any tough job that is handed to us and run away with it. The tougher the job, the better we'll like it.

2. Before a carrier can do its big job of sinking enemy ships, several hundred small unspectacular jobs have got to be done, and done well. One man falling down on a small job can "bitch the works" for the whole ship. So learn everything you can about your job during this precommissioning period. Pretty soon we will be out where it rains bombs and it will be too late to learn then.

Note: This ship will be employed on dangerous duty. We will either sink the enemy or get sunk ourselves, depending on how well we learn our jobs now and do our jobs later. *Anyone who prefers safer duty see me and I will arrange to have him transferred.*

D.V.G.

Of course our crew immediately nicknamed the ship the *Can Do*, and to this day, whenever I bump into old *Guadalcanal* sailors, they never call her anything else.

To match the output of the jeep carrier production line the Navy had to step up a production line for carrier crews. We had told Kaiser we didn't think he could deliver the goods. Our faces would have been very red indeed if he had delivered ships to us faster than we could man them.

We established a Precommissioning School at Bremerton in which each crew got about six weeks' training before boarding their ship. Most of the boys came to this school fresh out of boot camp where they had learned some of the basic facts of life about ships in general. Here, we taught them as much as we could, ashore, about our type of ship in particular.

They studied the plans of the ship; they rubbed elbows with many of the actual machines they would have to operate; they were organized into a ship's crew of thirteen divisions and began to get acquainted with the officers who would lead them into battle. The final week of their course was a cruise in Puget Sound on the *Casablanca,* CVE-55, and the first of the Kaiser ships. For most of our lads, this excursion in Puget Sound was their first voyage on salt water.

By this time several of the big carriers had been sunk out in the far Pacific, and these sinkings turned out to be a blessing in disguise, at least for us who were trying to form crews as fast as the ships were sliding down the building ways. The survivors of the big carriers were split up among the crews of the little ones, and in many cases they were the only men in our crews who had ever been aboard a carrier before. Not many big carriers got sunk, however, so these experienced hands were spread mighty thin among the fifty jeeps.

The mass production of crews at that school and the results which those crews accomplished highlight the fact that one of the greatest national assets of this country is the intelligence and adaptability of our youth. A modern ship is packed full of strange machinery, but young Americans learn how to operate machinery quickly. It comes natural to them to shoot guns, operate radar, and run boilers and engines. This is, of course, simply another aspect of our tremendous industrial potential.

As a part of their precommissioning training all of our crew went through the Navy's Fire Fighting School at Bremerton. This school, run by professional firemen, used what modern educators would call the practical rather than the academic method. They taught you how to fight fires by actually making you fight them all day long. They

51

had full-scale models of engine rooms, hangar decks, and various other parts of ships, in which they set every kind of fire imaginable. The students learned how to use all the newest fire fighting equipment and techniques, how to get into a blazing compartment using a fog nozzle as a shield; to rescue the people who were trapped; and to snuff out the fire. For the week that you were in the school you were just one jump ahead of being fried alive. They would put you in the far end of a gasoline-drenched compartment, light the thing off, and leave you to your own devices. The only way you could get out of there was to drive the fire out ahead of you, or get dragged out by the boys in the asbestos suits who watched through peepholes from the outside, ready to rush in in case you hadn't studied your lesson properly and passed out.

I thought it would be a good thing for me to go through this school. I will never be so naïve again! I was the first four-striper to appear at the school, and those professional smoke eaters gave me a worse hazing than I got as a plebe at the Naval Academy. They didn't give me a "hotfoot" —they cooked me to a crisp all over!

They put me on the nozzle end of the hose and smack in the hottest part of every fire they set. They put me in places where the Devil himself would have squawked about the heat, and would have gotten the hell out of there. Time and time again the only sensible thing to do was to throw that damned hose away and run. The only trouble was that my whole crew were right there watching me, and you can't throw away a hose and run in a dignified manner when the seat of your pants is practically on fire. So I just had to sweat it out, hoping that the boys in the asbestos suits would step in if necessary.

This training which the boys got at the Fire Fighting School paid off in a big way later. Some brisk fires got started on the *Guadalcanal* in the next year, fires which might have destroyed the ship. But we put them out. If the Navy had had that Fire Fighting School in 1941, we wouldn't have lost the *Lexington, Hornet, Wasp* and

Yorktown in 1942. Later in the war the *Bunker Hill, Essex, Hancock,* and *Franklin* extinguished blazing infernos much worse than the fires in those early ships, and lived to fight another day.

When the builders have finished with a new ship she is still an inanimate thing. Her hull is seaworthy, her engines are sound, and her gear is good, but you can't tell whether she is destined to become a proud and respected lady or a weak sister.

When her crew steps aboard, the ship comes to life. The skipper, the officers, and each man in the crew, all loan her a piece of their souls, to keep as long as they serve in her. These little pieces added together make up the soul of the ship and change her from so many tons of cold metal to a warm, living and breathing member of the seagoing community of ships.

Some people think that, despite all our modern scientific knowledge, man will *never* learn how to put life into inanimate matter. Seafaring men have been doing this for centuries.

We put the *Guadalcanal* in commission at Astoria, Oregon, on September 25, 1943. Lining up on the flight deck in our best blue uniforms, we read the orders, hoisted the commission pennant and colors, and bowed our heads while Father Weldon said a prayer. I addressed the crew and said the only thing that anyone could say in that spot —that if we didn't have the Presidential Unit Citation flying from our foretruck within a year, we would be unworthy custodians of the great name being entrusted to our care.

We piped down and hopefully set the watch. In less than a year we had our Presidential Unit Citation, but until Germany surrendered, it had a Top Secret label on it; so I had to settle for having it in the flag bag instead of at the foretruck.

The skipper of a new ship has an easy job if he sets his sails right. Ninety-nine per cent of the officers and crew take those four gold stripes which he wears at their face value. They want to be proud of the ship, and would rather brag about her than gripe. They feel the same way toward the skipper. All he has to do is to steer such a course that the ship's company retain their original high opinion of him.

One of the things the skipper should do is get up in front of his men every week or so and talk to them so they can get acquainted with him and find out firsthand what he is thinking about.

Many officers are bashful about doing this. But someday they may have to issue an order which will mean life or death to every man in their crew. They should talk to their crew at least often enough so that the sound of their voices will be familiar when the great day comes.

There are many things which the crew probably know, but which the Captain should tell them anyway. There are things which may seem trite when you read them in peacetime, but which it is important to say to a new and inexperienced crew who are about to get into a shooting war.

Before entering dangerous water for the first time, the Captain should tell his crew that it's perfectly natural to be scared when you go into battle; that everybody feels that way no matter how much gold braid he may or may not have on his arm, but that you just go ahead and do your stuff anyway. He should also tell them that if the ship gets hit, he intends to put out the fires, plug up the holes, pump out the water, and bring her back to port. No doubt the crew would assume this intention, but this makes it official. A few such things as this said early in the game may save the ship later on. The fate of all hands can easily depend on one man who sticks to his post, when he feels that he really ought to get the hell out of there, simply because he heard the skipper guarantee to bring that ship back to port, provided the water didn't get up any higher than the whistle.

Words are important, but actions are more important.

The Captain must show all hands, by what he does in addition to what he says, that he places the interest and welfare of that ship and crew above his own selfish interests.

If necessary, the skipper sticks his neck out for his crew. If the Admiral's staff has thoughtlessly scheduled ship movements which will deprive the crew of their proper leave, he goes to the Admiral and respectfully puts in a beef, even though he thinks that he will get smacked down for it.

As soon as the officers and crew know that the skipper will go to bat for them, the skipper can turn in if he wants to, and spend most of his time in his bunk. All hands will heave around and make him look good on any job that comes their way.

After you get your crew in this frame of mind, being captain of a ship is the best job in the Navy. An Admiral's job is nice work too—but ask any Admiral, "What was the high spot of your naval career?" and he'll get a faraway look in his eye and say, "Once when I was skipper of the . . ."

I wouldn't swap my cruise as skipper of the *Guadalcanal* for all the Admirals' stripes in the Navy. After you have commanded a ship like that one, no matter how many stars they put in your flag, you can't help but wish sometimes that you could haul that blue flag down and move up from the flag bridge to the pilothouse of the ship again. As skipper you are a working member of the team, but as Admiral you are apt to feel like an outsider kibitzing on the skipper's show. Halsey was one of the few Admirals who was able to retain the personal touch from the august isolation of the flag bridge.

I had a tower of strength in my executive officer, Commander Jesse Johnson. There are times when the skipper thinks the quickest way to get something done is to blow his top and raise hell. When this happens, if you have a steady-going and understanding exec like Jesse, he acts as a shock absorber, keeps the ship on an even keel, and

55

allows only enough of the fireworks to percolate down the line to accomplish the desired purpose. With a different type of exec, the skipper has got to keep his temper, or he can easily make the ship too hot to live in. But if he keeps it, he may get so hot inside himself that he is not fit company to have on board. With a man like Johnson around to take the curse off of it, an occasional blast of seagoing language from the bridge can blow the fog out of befuddled seamen's minds like an offshore wind clears a harbor. Jesse was exactly the right kind of exec for me, although I must confess that he deserves a Purple Heart with a lot of stars in it for the suffering he patiently endured when I didn't think we were winning the war fast enough.

Commander Johnson used to run a synthetic half-hour "radio" program each evening, using the ship's public announcing system. At 6:00 P.M. Jesse would broadcast the news of the day as per Lowell Thomas. Then he switched to the role of disc jockey and played half a dozen hot platters, regaling his listeners between records with facetious commercials for the ship's galley, laundry, and barbershop, or any other activity for which we could cook up plausible plugs. Despite the monopoly which these enterprises enjoyed, their commercials often made more sense than those you hear over our major networks.

The last fifteen minutes of this very popular program came to be known as "The Children's Hour." Jesse devoted this time to spinning yarns about the Navy, which usually carried some moral that would help us in our work. Sometimes he wound up with a tall tale about the early days of naval aviation when every flight was an adventure, and when getting back on the ground again all in one piece was a noteworthy feat. Those were the days when any landing that you could walk away from under your own power was regarded as a "good" one.

Naturally one of these yarns was the one which all old-timers will swear to on a stack of Bibles, and which most of us claim to have actually witnessed. It happened back in 1922 and concerns a character whom we will call Gyp Gilligan. Gyp had been flying landplanes around San Diego for about two years and then was sent up to San Francisco to bring a flying boat down to San Diego.

Arriving at San Diego, Gyp, following his accustomed route up the Strand, got into the landplane traffic circle, glided in over the hangars, and was leveling off to land that seaplane on the field when his co-pilot poured the soup to her, grabbed the yoke, and pointed over the side at the pontoons, indicating his disapproval of Gyp's intended procedure.

Gyp smiled sadly, took over again, and landed in the bay. As soon as they got tied up to the buoy, Gyp cut the switches, turned to the co-pilot and said, "Joe, I'm sorry about that business back there on the field; I just plumb forgot that we were in a seaplane."

So saying, Gyp stepped out of the cockpit and over the side—into water up to his neck!

Much water had gone under the bridge while naval aviation was growing from that era to 1943. In the early days the old *Langley* was our only carrier; now new carriers were coming by the dozen in job lots. Strangely enough the Kaiser jeeps were almost a throwback to the *Langley* type. They were about the same size and had only a few more knots speed. If you had cut the small island off the Kaiser class, any old-timer encountering a jeep at sea could easily have thought that the years had been rolled back and he was seeing the old "Covered Wagon" again.

Members of the original crew of a ship are known as "plank owners." This term, handed down to us from the days of sailing ships, signifies that each man in the first crew is supposed to own one of the planks in the ship's deck.

To make our homesick lads feel that they now had another home, and to boost their ego as seafaring men, we issued handsomely engraved plank owner's certificates to all hands. These certificates, addressed "To all sailors, wherever ye may be, and to all whales, porpoises, mermaids and other living things of the sea . . ." made our lads, just out of boot camp, feel that a little salt was beginning to accumulate on them.

All those Kaiser ships started off with the greenest and most inexperienced crews that ever put to sea. The average age of our lads was about twenty-one, and over eighty per cent of them had never seen salt water before. They didn't even know a lee scupper from a running bowline, even though they made up in willingness what they lacked in nautical know-how. You can teach our kids a lot about machinery in a school ashore but you can't put a seaman's squint into their eyes and a rolling gait into their walk. The open sea is the only classroom where you can do that.

One morning, soon after commissioning, I was passing the time of day with our chief boatswain's mate, one of our few real sailormen on board, who had some fifteen years of naval service behind him. I asked him what he thought of the draft of new seamen we had received from boot camp the day before. He took a dim view of them.

"Cap'n," he said, "I'd swap 'em all for a bucket of oily rags."

I knew what he meant. It can drive a skipper to distraction to watch a bunch of eager farmers and shoe clerks fumbling around with a hawser on a dock, or trying to hook on a whaleboat in a seaway. These are routine jobs on which real sailormen will simply set taut and hoist away. But when it comes to the really big, unusual jobs, sometimes inexperience can be an asset.

If you tell a bunch of old-timers, "We're going out next cruise and sink the *Tirpitz*," they are apt to look at you kind of funny and say, "The Old Man has finally blown his top and gone nuts."

A bunch of youngsters will say, "Okay, we're going out to sink the *Tirpitz*," and may go out and do it. That's the kind of a crew we had on the *Guadalcanal*.

PLANK OWNERS' CERTIFICATE

USS GUADALCANAL

TO ALL SAILORS AND AVIATORS
WHEREVER YE MAY BE — GREETINGS!
KNOW YE BY THESE PRESENTS THAT

DANIEL V. GALLERY

WAS A MEMBER OF THE ORIGINAL CREW WHICH COMMISSIONED THE
USS GUADALCANAL AND IS THEREFOR ENTITLED TO ALL THE RIGHTS
AND PRIVILEGES OF A PLANK OWNER ON SAID SHIP INCLUDING A CLEAR
AND UNENCUMBERED TITLE TO ONE PLANK IN THE FLIGHT DECK.

DATE OF COMMISSIONING
25 SEPT 1943

D.V.Gallery

CAPTAIN U.S. NAVY
COMMANDING

Our chief quartermaster shared the boatswain's lack of enthusiasm for his new helpers. One day I overheard him instructing one of his new apprentices on how to record the weather data on the rough logbook. The chief gave him quite a lecture on cloud forms, the barometer, the Beaufort scale of wind velocities, and methods of estimating the size of waves in logging the state of the sea. At the conclusion of this lesson in seafaring lore the youngster piped up: "Say, chief, I read somewhere that the waves are smaller during a heavy rain because the rain beats their tops down. How about that?"

I don't think the chief relished this embellishment to his instruction by a neophyte. He scornfully replied, "Yeah, that's right. Except it don't beat down the tops; it fills in between the troughs."

Our younger officers were just as inexperienced as the men. Some thought they ought to call their men by their first names, and to preface an order by the request, "How's to . . ." Others thought their only responsibility was to be brave on the day that we went into battle. They were all willing to do anything the United States expected of them, but they simply didn't know what division officers are supposed to do. Commander Johnson and I had to teach them.

The biggest lesson we tried to put across was that division officers must be leaders, and must feel a personal sense of responsibility for everything done by any man in their divisions. If one of their men does something good, a division officer has a perfect right to smugly claim some of the credit; when a man falls down on the job, the division officer must expect to share the blame, and must never alibi by saying, "That fellow is a no-good bum."

At one of our sessions with the division officers I reminded them of that dramatic scene in the movie about the British Navy, *In Which We Serve*. This scene brings out one of the fundamental facts of life about any properly run military outfit.

The skipper of the destroyer, around which the picture

is written, is called upon to mete out punishment to a young sailor who deserted his post in battle. The lad knows that his proper punishment is a general court-martial. But the skipper says, "Son, you have served in my ship since she went in commission, and I have had two years to teach you how a sailorman should behave. If *I* had done my duty properly during this time, it would have been impossible for you to desert your post. We are equally guilty."

I cited the U.S.S. *Redwing* to our officers. The *Redwing* was a harbor tug, a little bit of a spit kit—although I salute her stout heart when I say that. She showed up in Reykjavik, Iceland, in December, 1941, twenty-three days out from Argentina, Newfoundland, having clawed her way through the North Atlantic blizzard to get there. Whoever ordered her up to Iceland should have been court-martialed. She had no business outside the inner harbor of Boston in the wintertime, and she nearly foundered several times in the howling gales and mountainous seas she encountered. Her crew actually kept her afloat by bailing with buckets. I sat in the officers' club in Iceland and listened to her skipper's story of that voyage in popeyed amazement. When he finished, I asked, "Wasn't your crew scared stiff when they had to bail?"

"No," he said. "They were all pretty green, so I told them that bailing ship was a routine maneuver in the Navy!"

I must admit that there were times when *I* was the one who needed educating rather than my new officers, and when I should have gotten a swift kick in the pants instead of the loyal support of all hands, which I did get.

A skipper in his first command may be inclined to be intolerant of suggestions about how he should run his ship—at least *one* skipper that I know was so inclined. I brushed off several good ideas proposed by our young officers, probably because I hadn't thought of them first myself. I guess I was just reluctant to admit that I wasn't as farseeing and omniscient as a skipper is supposed to be.

Sometimes the skipper isn't really as sure of himself as he wants his people to think he is. I bow my head and say, "Mea culpa."

This is a late date to atone for my transgressions, but I hereby apologize to my young lads for the cavalier manner in which I dismissed some of their sound suggestions. I think they will find, if they think back, that most of them actually were adopted within a few days, although maybe I made it look like they were my ideas.

We spent the first couple of weeks after commissioning alongside the dock learning our way around in the ship, testing the machinery, and cleaning the smell of the beach out of her.

High on the list of lessons that our youngsters had to learn about the ways of the seagoing Navy was the importance of getting back from liberty on time. Most of them had spent their entire naval careers at training stations and receiving ships where things had been pretty ragtime, and where overstaying liberty and even jumping ship had been accepted as normal procedure. We had to take a round turn on those ideas and snub them up short. One night at the movies I told the crew the story about the sailor on the *Saratoga* who requested an extension of leave in the following air mail letter:

C.O., U.S.S. *Saratoga*
Dear Captain:

When I got home I found that my father's brick silo had been struck by lightning, knocking some of the bricks off the top. I decided to fix the silo, and so I rigged up a beam, with a pulley and whip at the top of the silo, and hoisted a couple of barrels full of bricks to the top. When I got through fixing the silo there were a lot of bricks left over.

I hoisted the barrel back up again, secured the line at the bottom, and then went up and filled the barrel with the extra bricks. Then I went down to the bottom and cast off the line.

Unfortunately, the barrel of bricks was heavier than I was and before I knew what was happening, the barrel started down and jerked me off the ground. I decided to hang on, and halfway up I met the barrel coming down and received a severe blow on the shoulder. I then continued on up to the top, banging my head against the beam and getting my fingers jammed in the pulley.

When the barrel hit the ground it busted the bottom, allowing all the bricks to spill out. I was now heavier than the barrel and so started down again at high speed. Halfway down I again met the barrel and received severe injuries to my shins. When I hit the ground I landed on the bricks, getting numerous painful cuts from the sharp edges.

At this point I must have lost my presence of mind because I let go of the rope. The barrel then came down and struck me another heavy blow on the head, putting me in the hospital for three days.

Respectfully request five days extension of leave.

JOHN DOE

I told the boys that unless they could top that one, they would just be wasting their time and mine trying to alibi being overleave.

When we sailed on our shakedown cruise, the muster report showed no stragglers.

On the day we went in commission we started a custom which was adopted by many of the ships that followed us. Every morning, right after colors when in port, or right after sunrise at sea, the boatswain's mate blew his pipe and passed the word, "Attention to morning prayer." All hands knocked off what they were doing for half a minute, uncovered, and faced the bridge while the padre said a brief prayer over the loud speaker.

As every Captain knows, the Creator of men's souls takes a hand at times in the destiny of his ship's soul. I had read several accounts of battles in the Pacific which told about holding special prayer services just before going into battle. When I discussed this with Father Weldon, we agreed that it was poor psychology, as well as bad theology, to wait until we were looking down the enemy gun barrels before starting to pray.

Besides that, Father Weldon quoted Mr. Dooley's famous remark: "Any healthy man, he sez, should be ashamed, he sez, to ask for help in a fight, he sez." So we got around that difficulty by asking for it every day as an item of ship's routine.

Whenever Father Weldon went on leave in between cruises he would write up a series of prayers, one for each morning that he would be gone, and would leave them with the officer of the deck.

Right after morning colors the O.O.D. would pinch-hit for the padre and read the prayer. In this manner every watch officer in the ship eventually had a turn at saying the morning prayer. Some of those officers hadn't been inside a church in ten years, to say nothing of ever leading a public prayer. But apparently the One to Whom the prayers were addressed made allowances for the exigencies of war, and our prayers were heard.

While thinking of spiritual needs, we didn't forget the physical ones. Napoleon's well-known remark about an army traveling on its belly applies equally well to a ship. A smart skipper pays just as much attention to what goes on in his galley and bakeshop as he does to the work on the bridge, combat information center, and the engine room.

Every sailor's contract with the government calls for three good square meals a day, and the skipper should see to it that his men get them. Thanks to the outstanding job done by our paymaster, Lieutenant Commander Stockenberg, there was no need to worry about this. I sampled the crew's ration every day, and often dropped in to the galley at unexpected times and snooped around looking for things that I could needle Stocky about, but he was

64

always a couple of jumps ahead of me. In fact, whenever we were in port, as soon as my boys had a chance to get ashore and do a little bragging about how they were eating, we used to have quite a number of gate crashers in our chow lines from ships at adjoining docks. I never objected to this because it gave me fine ammunition for ribbing the skippers of the other ships.

While we got the ship ready for sea, our air group lived ashore at a nearby air station. I preached one revolutionary idea to all hands in the ship's company right from the beginning: when our air group came aboard during the shakedown cruise I wanted them greeted as long-lost brothers, not as intruders. As a pilot in the peacetime Navy, I had seen air groups treated like illegitimate offspring at a family reunion on arrival aboard the carrier for duty. This was not going to happen on the *Guadalcanal*.

Air groups come and go on a carrier. When there is no air group aboard, it is perfectly natural for the regular ship's company to spread out and occupy the vacant living, office, and shop spaces intended for the air groups. When the air group comes aboard, the "squatters" have to move over to make room. This, plus the extra pay for the flyers and their exemption from routine watches, tends to cause friction between the air group and ship's company, when you have no foreign enemies to fight.

For some obscure reason the sailors in the air group are referred to by the ship's company as "airedales." They get fifty per cent extra pay for flying duty. One day I heard one of the ship's company arguing with an airedale about which one had the toughest job, and the argument broke up with this classic summation of the case: "Well, I can see how you airedales earn your fifty per cent flight pay, but what the hell do you do to earn the base pay?"

Before we even went in commission, we impressed on all hands that the only reason for the ship's existence was to fly airplanes, and that without our air group we were useless. We had five different groups while I was in the ship and never a complaint from any of them.

As the sailing date for our shakedown cruise drew near, we were making friends with our ship and beginning to know her and like her. You don't have to live very long in a ship to find out whether she is going to be a sweetheart or a shrew.

All sailors know that no two ships are alike. Even landlubbers know that a square-rigged windjammer is different from a steam vessel, a merchant ship from a man-of-war, and a battleship from a carrier. These differences are physical ones in the hulls, rigging and spars.

But long before the days of John Paul Jones, sailors were saying, "different ships—different long splices." What they were talking about was not the variety in the lines and frames of ships, in ground tackle and superstructures, not even in roll and pitch. What they meant was that every ship that sails the seas has its own individual personality and character.

Even identical sister ships like the Kaiser jeeps, built from the same set of plans, as alike physically as two swab handles, can be as different as day and night. One is happy, the other surly. One is lucky, the other never finds a fair breeze. One can go alongside a dock in a mean cross tide and a foul wind without knocking a splinter off a piling. The other will make a dozen powerful tugs puff and grunt to shove her alongside at slack water in a flat calm. You can bet your life on one in the wildest gale that blows, and the other is not to be trusted beyond the horizon.

A lot depends on how the ship starts life off on her shakedown cruise. If by good luck and good management you can steer through the first couple of weeks at sea without serious trouble, things just seem to drop into their proper places. From then on your crew gets accustomed to doing things right, success becomes normal, and you've got a smart ship in the making.

CHAPTER 4

SHAKEDOWN CRUISE

We cast off from the dock for our shakedown cruise in October, 1943. Just as we backed clear of our berth, a frantic call came up from the engine room: "We've got to stop the port engine. *You'd better get back alongside the dock!*"

What a lubberly way that would have been to start off on our maiden voyage. I yelled back into the squawk box, "Stop your engine, but get busy and fix it. We're going out on one screw."

Earl Trosino, our chief engineer, never called for time out again as long as he was in the ship. He kept that ship going in spite of blown-out boiler tubes, scored piston rods, bad brick work in the fire boxes, and salt in the feed water. On our return from every cruise that we later made in the Atlantic, the Navy Yard foreman came up to the cabin after inspecting our plant and told me, "You just barely made it this time. If you had to go another ten miles you would have been towed in." I never argued with him. But Earl and I both knew that the *Guadalcanal* could go wherever she had to go. Earl sweat blood at times, but we always made it.

That first night at sea my farmer boys received a tough initiation into the realm of Neptune. We crossed the bar of the Columbia River on the tale end of a northwest gale. The bar was breaking and whitecapped rollers swept in before the wind, which was still blowing great guns. The old girl started chomping at the bit as soon as she stuck her nose into it, and immediately proved that she knew how to heave and roll and pitch like a real ship. Before we had been out fifteen minutes we were taking green water aboard on the flight deck, and I'm sure most of my lads bitterly regretted that they hadn't joined the Army.

One alarming characteristic of our ship was dinned into our ears the moment we crossed the bar and got some motion on her. The thin plates between the hangar deck and the flight deck "oil canned" on every pitch of the ship, i.e. the plates would spring in when we were over the back of a wave and the plates were in tension, springing out when we got in the trough and put them under compression. This springing in and out like an oil can was accompanied by a thunderous booming that reverberated through the ship and reminded everybody of the predictions that these ships would break in two. Actually there was no danger of this, but that ominous thunder sounded like the crack of doom.

At one time during that first night we lost our fuel oil suction and wallowed heavily in the trough of the sea, for about ten minutes, with both our engines stopped. I don't mind saying I would rather forget those ten minutes. I didn't know how long it would take to get the engines going again and as we drifted toward the beach I began to wonder if the anchors would hold and keep us out of the surf. At times like that a skipper also wonders what foolish impulse ever made him follow the sea instead of taking up some quiet profession such as safecracking or race track gambling. Ten minutes like that should count for at least a year when they start figuring up your time toward retirement.

Our preliminary shakedown cruise took us to Puget Sound; we were slated to spend ten days doing the odd jobs which must be done to a ship just out of the builder's yard. However, we were eager beavers and feared that they might win the war without us if we didn't hurry. So we cut a lot of corners, worked late into the night, and finished all our jobs in five days.

After a full day's work on a Saturday we received an ammunition lighter alongside at 9:00 P.M., and worked till two o'clock Sunday morning getting the ammunition aboard and stowed. This was an all-hands job for the deck force. I was on the flight deck at midnight watching the boys hoist cargo nets full of bombs out of the lighter, trundle them over the deck and strike them below.

At the stroke of eight bells, music blared forth from the loudspeakers all over the ship. My seagoing disc jockey ushered in the Sabbath with *Praise the Lord and Pass the Ammunition.*

We took a few chances to finish our odd jobs quickly, such as running up and down the degaussing range in a fog while our only gyro compass was under repairs. Some seamen will call this a "miscalculated risk"; but we got away with it, and I figured it was important for *me* to put the "Can Do" idea into action as well as words. The crew are quick to notice whether the skipper himself will do the kind of things he is asking them to do.

However, one thing we almost didn't get away with was upsetting the apple carts of some of the feather merchants ashore in the Operations Department of the Naval District Headquarters, by our early departure. We revised our schedule faster than they could keep up with us, while discharging their social duties around Seattle. So when we finished all our jobs five days ahead of time and radioed that we were on our way to San Diego, they couldn't get a blimp out in time to escort us, as required by Sea Frontier regulations. I didn't want the blimp anyway, because I figured the only thing it could do was to mark our position conspicuously and attract submarines. I learned later that some of the higher-ups on the Naval District Staff recommended me to be keelhauled for my unseemly haste. But the Admiral took a more tolerant view and said, "When a man's in a hurry to get to war, the best thing to do is to speed him on his way."

We took advantage of this period in Puget Sound to learn the maneuvering characteristics of our ship and to train our young officers in ship handling. Like learning to drive a new car, there are a lot of things about handling a new ship that you have to find out by experiment. How much room does it take to turn her with different amounts of rudder? What will she do if you back your inboard engine after slamming your rudder hard over in a tight spot? How far will she forge ahead after you throw both engines full astern trying to avoid a collision? We backed and filled all over Puget Sound, with all deck officers on the bridge, finding out that the Kaiser jeeps are the sweetest-handling class of ship you've ever seen.

Everybody took turns being "Captain" while we heaved boxes overboard pretending they were submarine periscopes, and learned how to ram them with our stem, a procedure which isn't as easy as it sounds. Other boxes represented lifeboats. Everybody had a shot at laying the ship alongside with the wind abeam without bumping them, and within reach of a heaving line.

The skipper takes a real interest in this kind of school-teaching because a Captain's reputation is often in the hands of his officers of the deck. The O.O.D. runs the ship when the skipper is not on the bridge and his handling of the ship reflects the training which the Captain has given him. The Captain is, of course, responsible for what the O.O.D. does. If the Officer of the Deck performs a lubberly maneuver which makes the ship look clumsy to the rest of the task group, the Captain will, naturally, put the blast on the offender. However, if the Admiral later gets the skipper on the carpet about it and inquires the name of the O.O.D., the only proper reply is, "I had the deck, sir."

When a bunch of seafaring men are swapping yarns you can usually pick out a skipper from the others just by listening for the pronouns they use. The others, in lying about their adventures, will say, *"We* rounded Cape Horn in a howling gale. . . . We threaded our way through icebergs a mile high. . . ." The skipper will say, "I clawed my way around the Cape. . . . I battened down the hatches and pooped the deck. . . ." Frequently a skipper, when speaking of another ship, will say "he" did so-and-so, instead of "she." He is thinking of the other skipper when he does this.

No seafaring man would even think of attributing this to egotism on the skipper's part. It stems quite naturally from the elementary facts of life at sea. The skipper makes the final decisions, holds the sack, and sweats out many a night watch wondering whether he is right or wrong. He can get plenty of advice about everything he does, but in theory at least he will reject all the bad advice—otherwise he wouldn't be skipper. If he loses his ship he will have to say "I" when he testifies before the court-martial, even though disaster was the fault of his subordinates. So why shouldn't he say "I" when he is astounding his listeners around a bottle?

In case of emergency, the O.O.D. sometimes can't wait for the Captain to get up to the bridge and must act on his own initiative. I told my lads that if they *acted* when action was required and what they did turned out to be wrong, I would take the rap. But if they were still wringing their hands and trying to make up their minds what to do when failure to act brought about disaster, then I would probably spend my time wringing my hands and wondering how to help them when we got court-martialed.

Another officer on whom the Captain must rely very heavily is his navigator. Our navigator, Jan Bikkers, was a graduate of the Dutch Naval Academy in Holland, but he had given up seafaring and come over here after World War I. Our first day at sea I caught him working out a sun sight, using a Dutch book printed back in 1910.

I told him if I ever saw that book again, I would heave it overboard and heave him after it. If we ran aground we would do it using official U.S. Navy publications—not any foreign substitutes.

Of course, if you ever do run a ship aground there isn't a thing in the world the skipper can say except, "Oops— I'm sorry. I didn't do it on purpose!" No matter what the circumstances, if the skipper tries to alibi and put the blame on his navigator—or anyone but himself—he just

71

makes himself look ridiculous. There is no other job in the world where one man has unquestioned authority and full responsibility so clearly fixed on his shoulders alone. The Captain of a ship enjoys many rights and privileges. He pays for them by accepting an inescapable responsibility for the safe navigation of the ship.

Our quartermaster's gang must have thought Bikkers and I were both balmy. I told him one day I would never consider him a real navigator until he got us a fix by crossing a sun line with Venus in broad daylight.

If you are patient enough and know exactly where to look for it, you can find Venus even at high noon in certain seasons of the year. But finding it and bringing it down to the horizon in a sextant are two different things. Often on clear days one or the other of us would suddenly yell: "There she is," point to an apparently empty patch of blue sky, and bring the quartermasters scrambling out of the chart house with sextants, stop watches and notebooks. But we never got our fix.

Bikkers never really became reconciled to navigating a carrier. A very methodical Dutchman, he liked to lay his courses out on the chart for many hours in advance. Very often just as he got his advanced dead reckoning figured out to a quarter of a degree and neatly laid down on the chart, something unexpected would happen and we would go chasing the wind all around the compass to launch or land aircraft, thus completely fouling up his calculations. I know he still suspects that several alleged emergency landings were cooked up for the sole purpose of making him rub out his handiwork and do it all over again.

Bik had firmly fixed opinions about many subjects, and didn't mind airing them in the ward room. One of his pet peeves was the barnyard morals of some members of the movie colony in Hollywood. One member of the mess was a reserve officer who was also a very successful member of this colony. He took exception to Bik's tirades, and at a later date, when we were docked in Panama, he decided to expose Bik as a hypocrite and a fraud.

Letting about a half a dozen of the boys in on his conspiracy, he got up a party to explore the night life of Panama, and included Bik in the party. The party repaired to a well-known cabaret on the Pacific side of the Isthmus, engaged a table, and, of course, a bevy of hostesses immediately moved in.

Bik's friend from Hollywood called the snappiest-looking number of the bunch aside and gave her twenty bucks to go to work on Bik, with the understanding that if she got him into bed with her there would be another twenty in it for her. Meantime numerous bets were placed by the other members of the party on the outcome of this test, the odds varying with the confidence or lack of it which the betters had in Bik.

Bik knew nothing about all this. All he knew was that a sultry female fell for him like a ton of bricks and made quite a pass at him. He was quite flattered and joined in the spirit of the occasion—up to a certain point. But that was all. After an hour of eager, conscientious effort the chagrined young temptress finally gave up, and the boys who had bet on Bik collected, some of them getting a nice price.

Bik was the hero of the mess the next day. He still didn't know what the score actually was, and he was becomingly modest about the whole thing. But his prowess as a Lothario was the principal topic of conversation.

Two days later another assault on his virtue was organized. This time about a dozen of his messmates were in on the deal. They selected the hottest babe in the floor show of the leading cabaret in Colon, and raised the ante to fifty bucks down and fifty bucks bedside.

Large sums of money were wagered again, because although on past performance Bik had shown real class, his opposition this time was championship caliber. She was billed as a former Follies gal, and so her backers had to lay pretty long odds to get their money covered. In fact some of the horse players in the crowd were inclined to regard the event as a "boat race."

The lady put up a good solid contest. She was a competent craftsman, with form, experience, and interest in her work. She turned on the heat and used every seductive wile of the trade. After the preliminary sparring was over, there wasn't another cent of Bikkers' money in sight. In the closing rounds along toward midnight she had him hanging over the ropes, and it didn't seem possible that he could finish on his feet. But he did, and all hands caught the twelve-thirty boat back to the ship.

Next day Bik was the smuggest, the most self-satisfied Lieutenant Commander you've ever seen. When the first dame made passes at him, he had figured it was just one of those things and that maybe he reminded her of someone else. But when the toast of the Canal Zone spun in over him then he began thinking maybe he must have charms which even he had not appreciated up to that time. His ego inflated quite understandably, and the awed hero-worship of his messmates pumped it up to the bursting point.

Then some low character let the cat out of the bag and exposed the whole business to Bik. Do you think this busted the balloon? You don't know Bik if you think so! Most people would have gotten quite angry and perhaps have wound up with an inferiority complex—but not Bik. He simply switched his line of reasoning and instead of flattering himself on his sex appeal he took refuge in righteous satisfaction at his strength of character.

So his ego was lifted to even greater heights. And if you ask me I'd say it had a damned good right to be. In fact, if I had been in Bik's shoes, I would have demanded at least ten per-cent cut from all the winners in this bawdy parley.

But I've gotten a little ahead of my story. . . . When we arrived in San Diego we hoisted our air group aboard alongside the air station dock and put to sea again to cut our teeth as an aircraft carrier.

In the previous three weeks our baby flattop had developed from a potential menace to navigation into a ship with reasonably good sea manners. We were, by now, at least apprentices in the ancient order of seamen. Overnight we were expected to become experts in the ultramodern guild of that order which puts wings on seamen and sends them soaring aloft. Maybe we were still a little bit lubberly about things that Columbus' sailors could do while standing up in a hammock. But we were now about to do things that would make Noah shake his head and say: "The Navy ain't what it used to be."

I was determined to make the first take-off and landing on the ship. I knew that it might cost me a little bit of sweat, but the advantages to be gained by it would be out of all proportion to the effort involved. It would give me a license to say things to the air group commander which I would have no right to say otherwise.

There wasn't a puff of wind blowing on the morning that we received our baptism as a carrier. All that we had to work with on the flight deck was the wind we were able to make with our own engines; about eighteen knots. As the scheduled time for take-off approached, Joe Yavorsky, our air group commander, came up to the bridge and recommended that we delay operations until a breeze sprang up, saying, "Of course, you can't land with less than twenty-five knots on a little ship like this."

"Okay, Joe," I said. "Call off operations for your boys till we get enough wind."

Then I went aft on the flight deck, climbed into my plane, took off, made one trip around the ship, and landed. Yarvorsky met me rather sheepishly as I got out of the plane, and said his boys were ready to go.

This paid off in a big way later on. Plenty of times after we got into the war we had to operate with no wind. But nobody ever came up to the bridge to beef about the lack of wind from that day on.

Two years later, on my first day in command of the great carrier *Hancock,* I was standing on the bridge as flight operations were about to begin, surveying the vast expanse of her flight deck and mentally comparing her with the *Guadalcanal*. I was thinking of our night operations from that tiny postage stamp of a deck, sometimes with only fifteen knots of wind.

My meditations were rudely interrupted by the Air Officer who asked me to please get a little more speed on the ship, pointing out that we only had twenty-five knots of wind across the deck. I'm afraid that for a new skipper, just moving up to the big leagues, my reply was a bit on the abrupt side, and that I acquired a reputation that morning, with the Air Department, for being a hard man.

We took time out from flight operations on that first day on the *Guadalcanal* to practice another maneuver that wasn't listed among the things we were supposed to do, but which paid off later. We told our destroyer plane guard to stop her engines and then steamed up alongside her, passed her an inch and a quarter wire cable, and took her in tow.

I'm sure none of my people could see much point in doing this extra job which entailed a lot of backbreaking heaving and hauling on heavy gear. But I was nursing a hope—a hope so far-fetched and improbable of achievement that I didn't feel like explaining it to anyone at that time. But our knowledge of handling a tow line was to stand us in good stead less than a year later when a dream came true and we hit the jackpot off the coast of French West Africa.

Henry Monat, our senior medical officer, born and educated in France, was a fabulous character. I could write a book about him, but nobody would believe it. He spoke nearly all modern languages fluently, and, I might add, almost continuously.

He thoroughly understood that one of the principal duties of the ship's doctor is to take proper care of the wounded. His plans for handling battle casualties were fantastic. He must have figured that we were going to fight our way into Tokyo Bay singlehanded, and that by the time we got in there, he and I would be the only ones left on our feet. I finally had to tell him that any time

76

the stretcher cases filled up the hangar deck and began to overflow onto the flight deck, we would withdraw from the battle, temporarily, until he could get the situation squared away again.

One day, early in our career, a hospital apprentice came rushing up to the bridge and announced: "Doctor Monat says stop the ship!" It seems that Henry had an emergency appendicitis case on his hands and was getting ready to operate. We adjusted course and speed so as to get the least roll and pitch, and Henry went to work. About a half-hour later he came bursting up to the bridge himself, with a well-satisfied professional smile on his face and a bundle of gauze in his hands.

"Captain," he said, "I got it just in time. Look . . ." and he opened the gauze and shoved a gangrenous appendix right under my nose. He damned near got *my* appendix right back in his face.

I was bitterly disappointed when the order came in, about this time, assigning the *Guadalcanal* to the Atlantic. After my year and a half up in Reykjavik I figured I had served my time in that ocean and should be eligible for parole to the Pacific, where the fighting was much more exciting than the monotonous grind of anti-submarine warfare.

Our assignment to the Atlantic turned out to be a very lucky break indeed. Out in the Pacific CVE's were small cogs in a big machine and were used mostly as transports for hauling replacement aircraft to Admiral Halsey's fast carrier task forces, except for that one fateful morning at the battle of San Bernardino Strait when they acted as scarecrows for MacArthur's helplessly exposed forces in Leyte Gulf, and frightened off Admiral Kurita's battleships. For an hour that morning the fate of the Philippine campaign hung in the balance. When Kurita turned and ran from what he thought were Essex class carriers, he made one of the most colossal blunders in naval history, a blunder which justified that whole building program in the Kaiser yard even if the jeep carriers never did anything else. If Kurita had simply put his head down, kept swinging both fists, and plunged ahead he could have:

a) Sunk all our jeep carriers who came within range;

b) Decimated our amphibious fleet in Leyte Gulf;

c) Returned to Japan as a conquering hero via Suriago Strait, which was guarded only by our old battleships.

These ships had just fought the historic Battle of Suriago Strait, *and were out of ammunition!*

But that was the exception to the rule in the Pacific where the jeeps usually were very small fish in a big pond. In the Atlantic they were the big fish in the pond. There was plenty of sea room, and the CVE's still had a big job to do in clinching the victory over the U-boats.

Our shakedown cruise took us from San Diego to Norfolk via the Panama Canal, gave us a chance to get our sealegs, and to get accustomed to the routine of life at sea. This can be either a very humdrum existence or a daily adventure, depending on how the sailor concerned is put together.

The daily routine of a ship is as standardized as that of an Army post. You get up, eat, stand watch, and turn in at night according to a set schedule, subject to only minor changes by the plan published each morning for that particular day. But even the plan of the day doesn't specify whether the next ship that heaves up over the horizon will be a rusty tramp with *Singapore* lettered on her stern, a sleek packet out of Rio, or the *Queen Mary*. To some of your men these are all just passing ships. Other lads can lean on the rail and watch them go from one horizon to the other dreaming of faraway lands, strange people and high adventure.

The fifteen hundred men in your crew are just so many names and rates in the watch quarter and station bills posted on the bulletin boards throughout the ship. Line them up in ranks on the flight deck and they all look pretty much alike. But their life stories and characters are all different, and their various ambitions, good deeds and sins would fill many volumes.

You can serve in a large ship for a year and still meet a stranger every day. While you are in a ship you can make some lifelong friends, or you can leave her at the end of your cruise no richer in real friendship than you were when you came aboard.

The sea itself is ever-changing. When in a turbulent mood, its howling gales and mountainous breaking waves make the stoutest ship seem a frail refuge from the wrath of nature. I've felt a great ship tremble like a little airplane hitting a bump, when she smashed into a great storm wave and tons of green water crashed aboard flinging geysers of solid snow-white spray higher than the masts. "Laboring heavily" is the proper nautical way to describe her motion in the log when the rollers batter her from side to side and you wonder if she will recover from the next roll. Sleep is impossible because you have to hang onto the sides of your bunk to keep from being spilled out when she wallows in a trough. I suppose the biggest storm wave ever seen didn't measure over one hundred feet from trough to crest, but those kinds of waves are perhaps fifteen hundred feet from one crest to the next one. They are crowned with breaking surf, their backs are shaggy with vivid white wind streaks, and the seething spume rising from them makes it seem as if the sea is coming to a boil.

But after the storm has blown itself out and the sea's mood is peaceful, it becomes a broad highway over which even the outrigger canoes of the Polynesians traveled safely from Samoa to Honolulu.

Each day at sea you have a sunrise and sunset different from any others there have ever been before. Each night the cavalcades of stars march overhead, never changing but always new—because one lifetime is too little time to know them all. If you are alive to these varieties of life at sea, each day can be a new experience; if you are not, it's just "another day, another dollar," although this time-honored phrase understates the present-day sailor's pay by about 400%.

Reveille at sea is at 0600, for all hands except those who had the midwatch. We still call it "up all hammocks" in the Navy, instead of reveille, even though hammocks disappeared from our ships some years ago. The masters at arms go around the ship raising hell, hurling insults into every compartment, and treating it as open mutiny if any dopey sailor is a little bit slow in crawling out of his sack. In the not too distant past the deck force used to put an edge on their appetites between reveille and breakfast by scrubbing down all weather decks with holystones. Pushing one of these porous bricks around the sanded deck with a swab handle used to be one of the common denominators in all sailors' memories of life at sea. We don't do it any more in aircraft carriers for several reasons. In the first place, trying to scrub the oil, grease, and tracks of skidding tires from the vast expanse of a flight deck, would be like trying to sweep all the sands out of the Sahara Desert before breakfast. In the second place, while a properly scrubbed deck is the apple of an old seaman's eye, a holystoned flight deck would stand out like a sore thumb to an enemy scouting plane. So we now commit what any old-timer would regard as a sacrilege by painting the flight deck battleship gray. The old-timers would probably take their chances with the enemy bombs, rather than be party to such a lubberly outrage.

At 0800 each morning you hold quarters for muster. Every man must be accounted for every day. You may wonder why we insist on an accurate check every day at sea, where there is no other place for people to go. But there is *one* place where a man can go, and we have to notify his next of kin if he goes there. After muster, special orders for the day are published and there is a ten-minute period of setting-up exercises—otherwise known as "monkey drill." The rest of the forenoon is usually devoted to general drills at battle stations, and, of course, on a carrier you have airplanes taking off and landing periodically to keep all hands on the flight deck and hangar deck busy.

Most ships now feed the crew on the cafeteria system, but until World War II they stuck to the time-honored ritual of having the mess cooks set the tables and bring the food from the galley, and of piping the whole crew to mess simultaneously as a military maneuver. It took the advent of aircraft carriers where mealtimes have to be adjusted to flight schedules to break the old seagoing tradition of piping to meals on the bell.

I'll never forget one day fifteen years ago when my squadron was based on the *Ranger*, before we broke this tradition. We were sent out that morning on a scouting problem, and in accordance with standard practice, the problem was laid out so that we could get back to the ship with one hour's reserve of gasoline. The air group of some seventy planes swarmed around the ship at the end of the problem a few minutes before noon, ready and anxious to land. Promptly at eight bells the *Ranger* piped the crew to dinner and left us circling around up there for the next hour while her people went down below and stuffed their guts.

When they finally brought us aboard at 1300, there was the closest approach to a mutiny that I've ever seen in the U.S. Navy. Not long after that all carriers adopted the cafeteria system of feeding.

There is usually no set routine for the afternoons at sea. Most of your crew stand one watch in three; which accounts for eight hours out of every day. Those not on watch in the afternoon are employed on the hundreds of odd jobs that must be done to keep things shipshape. In the present-day Navy there is a lot of scrubbing down of bulkheads with soap and water. In prewar days we used to paint the bulkheads every time we happened to think of it, and, as a matter of fact, sailors will paint the whole ship every day if you let them. Tom Sawyer would have loved the prewar Navy.

But although plastering a ship with paint whenever

you have a few idle hours will keep her looking like a yacht, it will also make her burn like a shingle factory if she gets hit. We learned this to our sorrow early in World War II, and quit slinging paint around.

Our ships used to be full of bright work, which was very nice to look at, and which took a lot of elbow grease to keep shined. But well-shined bright work on the top-side reflects sunlight even better than a holystoned flight deck, so even the bright work is now painted, too.

I made just one concession to the old tradition of bright work, by demanding that the ship's bell be kept properly shined. I'm sure that the ship's cooks thought I was haz-ing them and felt very badly used indeed when they had to come all the way up from the hangar deck and shine the bell in the signalmen's bailiwick up by the bridge. But in sailing-ship days the ship's bell used to hang just outside the galley, and it was the traditional job of the cooks to keep it shined.

In off-duty hours the boys have many ways to amuse themselves. Most ships have a hobby shop, library, and crew's reading room. A very popular seagoing pas-time is acey-deucy—the nautical version of backgammon. Everybody in the Navy claims that he is a champion at this game for some large area—such as the Atlantic Ocean.

Craps is of course a popular game too. But aboard ship crap games must be of the "floating" variety—literally as well as figuratively. If the master at arms finds a crap game he confiscates all the money in sight for the welfare fund, and writes up all the participants for Captain's mast.

Aboard ship the movies are always well-attended no matter what kind of a stinkeroo of a picture you have. The boys will turn out in large numbers for a turkey just to hoot and jeer. All films circulate through the fleet in accordance with a schedule arranged by the Navy Movie Exchange, and ships at sea in a task group are supposed to exchange films whenever they come alongside for fuel or provisions. But a black market in good films grew up in the Pacific. When a destroyer with a red hot Betty

Grable film came alongside a carrier for fuel, they would demand two stinkeroos and fifty gallons of ice cream before they would part with their prize.

A very simple gag will sometimes keep a ship's company amused for a week. Once on the *Langley,* when we were about to cross the equator back in 1937, we published a memo to all hands requesting them to make certain personal observations on the day we crossed the line. This memo pointed out that hurricanes, cyclones, and whirlpools all rotate counter-clockwise in the northern hemisphere and clockwise in the southern. (This well-known phenomenon is caused by the rotation of the earth.)

The memo went on to state that scientists and medical men had been theorizing for years that this same reversal of twist when crossing the equator should occur in a small squirted stream of water. We requested that all hands take careful observations when we crossed the line, using whatever equipment was most convenient for the purpose, and report the results.

I regret to say that our investigation produced no valid scientific data. It stirred up heated discussion all over the ship, but the boys all seemed to take a frivolous attitude toward the experiment and none of the hundreds of reports submitted were suitable for quotation in this book. However, there was a great deal of argument about the matter; quite a lot of money was bet; and on the day we crossed the line, I believe everybody in the ship made a couple of trips below to check up.

The *Mission Bay,* a sister ship, accompanied us on our cruise from San Diego to Norfolk. On the way to Panama the Army asked us to play war with them and challenged us to test out the air defense of the Canal. I don't think the defenders of the Big Ditch took our little jeep carriers too seriously when they arranged this game. The things we did to their radar warning net, their interceptors and bombers were as illegal as piracy.

Their far-flung air scouting line picked us up five hundred miles from the Canal, just before sunset, and they kept a shadower over us all night. By prearrangement, we parted company with the *Mission Bay* right after dark. She made a beeline for the Canal, while we backtracked to the north for Salinas Bay in Nicaragua. The shadower, unfortunately, elected to stay with the *Guadalcanal,* but, by judicious skullduggery, we made that plane think we were steaming south all night when we were actually running north. You have to behave very dishonestly to do that.

We got our shadower's navigation so badly fouled up that the plane sent out to relieve him, just before sunrise, found nothing but an empty ocean several hundred miles to the southward of our actual position. I am sure that no one in the Air Force who was on duty in Panama at that time will ever trust the Navy again, even under oath.

You understand, of course, that this deception was a bit complicated, otherwise we couldn't have fooled our brothers-in-arms as we did. However, I will try to explain it so that even an Air Force pilot can understand it.

It all hinges on two simple facts: First, that on a dark night you can't tell looking down on the rectangular flight deck of a carrier whether she is headed north or south. The only way you can tell is by spotting the bow wave at one end and the wake coming off the other. Second, that an aviator flying a complicated pattern over a ship, which is making good a known course and speed, bases his navigation on this "known" course and speed of the ship rather than on an independent plot of his own gyrations.

When our friend found us at sunset we were headed south and he knew and reported our exact position, course, and speed. Then he began flying a clover-leaf pattern over us, keeping track of us by radar. We soon found that this clover-leaf pattern brought him back over us only once every half-hour.

I knew that if I had been in that plane I would not have attempted to lay down this complicated clover-leaf pattern on my chart and to keep a dead reckoning plot of my position. I would have started from the known fix at the first contact, and every hour during the night, while the ship held the same course and speed, I would have moved her twenty miles further south on my chart. So I made the conservative assumption that our Air Force pilots are no smarter than Navy pilots.

The problem was to make him think we were running south all night when we were actually going *north!* We did this by tampering with the bow wave and the wake.

Shortly after dark, when our friend was out of visual contact and just after *Mission Bay* sheared out, we reversed course and steamed north the rest of the night. Every time the shadower's clover leaf brought him back over us we backed full speed. This put the "bow" wave on the south end of the ship and made a "wake" coming off the north end, indicating that we were still running south at twenty knots. In the phosphorescent waters around Panama this was "unmistakable" from the air.

We couldn't actually turn south and then north again because two 180° turns require about five minutes, and would have left a conspicuous S-shaped trail in the luminescent water showing exactly what we were doing.

(Do you "follow" me so far? . . . So did our Air Force friend, who escorted us all night.)

He simply moved his charted position ten miles further *south* every half-hour. Actually we were making good about seven and a half miles to the *north* every thirty minutes, but homing on us by radar it was very easy to miss this.

Just before daylight he had to leave us, but he confidently radioed our position to his relief before shoving off. His "relief" hasn't found us yet because the position was about three hundred miles in error.

Next day we pulled a Statue of Liberty play on the Canal defenses. *Mission Bay* launched her planes with orders to climb way up in the air on the Pacific side, where the Canal Zone radars would be sure to "see" them.

Simultaneously the *Guadalcanal's* bombers cut across the Isthmus of Nicaragua, above the Canal, stayed down low, and hit the Gatun Dam coming in from the *Atlantic* side.

The play went for a touchdown. All the fighter defenses of the Canal tackled *Mission Bay's* decoys on the Pacific side, and our bombers went the length of the field to the Gatun Dam unopposed. I could write a chapter about how this proves the Navy's case for mobile carrier bases—but I won't.

The Canal Zone scouts didn't find the *Guadalcanal* again until near the end of the afternoon watch that day. By that time we were committed to arrive in Panama at a definite hour, so we held our course and speed all night with no hocus-pocus.

We knew that after sunrise the guardians of the Canal would lower the boom on this troublesome little insect of ours, which had fouled up their defenses.

Just before sunrise, we met an angry rain squall about five miles in diameter. I sent for our aerological officer and said, "Riggs, for the next few hours you are the skipper of this ship. Put us right smack amidship of that squall and keep us there."

Riggs did a scientific job. For the next three hours weather conditions on our flight-deck were zero zero, although it was clear and unlimited a few miles away all around us.

Two squadrons of B-17's came out from Panama shortly after sunrise to beat the daylights out of us. They had our exact position, but the rain squall was a little too rich for their blood.

For three hours we watched them circling on our radar scope as they went round and round the mulberry bush waiting for us to come out. It was the most beautiful rat race I've ever seen in my life.

Finally we heard the two squadron commanders cooking up a deal on the radio to "get this damned thing over with," and to have their planes make individual instrument approaches by radar at one-minute intervals.

That meant that the jig was up—except that there had been a great deal of uninhibited chatter on the radio during the previous three hours. We had been listening in on this party line and by this time we knew all the radio call signs, authenticators, and procedure.

We simply called the two squadron commanders, using the "phone number" of their home base in Panama, and told them: "Exercise completed, return to base."

It so happens that both squadron commanders missed our transmission. But somebody *always* gets the word to knock off a tedious exercise. The number two and three planes promptly relayed the message to their skippers, thus making it seem all the more authentic. They all buzzed off and went home.

After we anchored in Panama the next day there was a critique of the exercise in General Brett's Headquarters. Adding insult to injury, I brought to this gathering a wire recording of all the radio transmission, climaxed by our phony about returning to base.

As soon as the critique was over, I slipped my cable and beat it right back to the ship. I'll never go ashore in Panama again as long as I live without a bodyguard. Some of those Air Force people might still be on duty there. Of course, now that we are unified, maybe this couldn't happen again.

There was an incident of our stay in Panama which might have cost me command of my ship if news of it had ever gotten home. A medical officer whose zeal exceeded his judgment by several hundred per cent, issued an order that every sailor returning from liberty must report to sick bay immediately upon his return, and take venereal prophylactic treatment. This came out in the form of an official ship's order to which no exceptions were to be allowed. It was a cut-and-dried proposition— if you went ashore, you *had* to take the treatment.

A more outrageous violation of individual rights is hard to imagine. To further complicate what might perhaps be called a delicate situation to begin with, this order was issued *after* the first liberty party was already ashore.

When the liberty party returned at midnight and were met at the gangway by this officious medico bent on enforcing his Hitler-like order, there was trouble. The vast majority of the liberty party were sober, and had spent their time ashore sightseeing and behaving themselves. Despite their outraged protests, they were marched down to sick bay, lined up, and given the works.

Next day the ship was red hot. Mutiny seethed on the hangar deck. Of course this was a flagrantly illegal order, and in the military service you are not bound to obey an illegal order. But most of my inexperienced lads didn't know enough about military law to understand their rights in a matter of this kind. And besides that, if you refuse to obey an order because you are conscientiously convinced that it is illegal, and it turns out that you were mistaken in your belief, the penalty for being wrong is very severe.

Fortunately Father Weldon got word of the boiling resentment and soon found out what it was all about. I'm afraid that when he did, the good father may have used some profane and slightly obscene language. He went to Jesse Johnson immediately, and as respectfully as possible demanded cancellation of the order.

At first Johnson tried to defend the order. It had been cooked up when he had been busy with other things and he had approved it without fully realizing what it meant. But he didn't like to cancel an order under pressure the day after approving it.

He and Father Weldon had some hot words. Finally Father Weldon broke out the Navy Regulation book, and assisted by all the legal talent he could find in the ward room, drew up an official letter of protest addressed to me via the executive officer. By the time this document was handed to him Jesse appreciated the gravity of the situation. So he canceled the order and Father Weldon withdrew the official letter.

All this happened unbeknownst to me until the day after we left Panama, when Jesse rather shamefacedly gave the whole story. I was a difficult man to get along with for the next couple of days. People avoided me as much as possible. I got that medico up to the cabin and blasted every square inch of his hide off. I should have hung him from the starboard main yardarm.

If any of my sailors had written home about this I don't think I would be writing this book now. I would have been yanked out of my command forthwith—and quite properly so.

Of course I knew nothing about this order and would never have sanctioned it if I had known. But it happened on my ship. It was my duty to indoctrinate all officers of that ship so they wouldn't think of doing such stupid things; to organize the ship so that such an order could not be issued without my knowledge; and to supervise what went on in the ship closely enough so that I would soon find out if such a blunder were committed. For failure in all these respects it would have been my duty to take the rap.

But I was lucky and caught this blooper in time. I was always lucky in that ship.

As we shoved off from Colon on the Atlantic side of the Canal and struck out into the Caribbean, the tempo of the war changed for us. The blood pressure and heart beat of everyone on board went up a couple of points.

You never worried about submarines in the Pacific. One of the big errors in Jap naval strategy was their failure to use their submarines offensively. But as soon as the Colon breakwater light dropped out of sight astern you were in waters where submarines might be lurking anywhere, ready to strike without warning. You had to get used to living with the idea that a torpedo could blow your bottom out at any hour of the day or night.

We steamed through the N.E. trades in the Caribbean, took the windward passage into the Atlantic, and coasted up past Hatteras and into the Virginia Capes without sighting anything more hostile than a school of porpoises.

Enroute to Hatteras we passed a few miles offshore of the spot where Columbus first landed on San Salvador. During the intervening years man had learned to build better ships, had developed more deadly weapons, and had converted a virgin continent into a great industrial nation. But if Columbus could have seen our submarine lookouts scanning the ocean with their glasses and the loading crews standing by their guns, he might have concluded that man had learned very little in those 451 years about how to run the world he lives in.

CHAPTER 5

PILGRIMAGE TO WASHINGTON

When we got to Norfolk I was called up to Washington for consultation with the Anti-Submarine Warfare experts in the Navy Department. I was "processed" through the system, "briefed" and "indoctrinated." After being duly checked to see if I was a good security risk I was allowed to enter the holy of holies where the daily plot of convoy and submarine movements was kept. After a couple of busy days up there I gratefully returned to my little ship.

No story of the seagoing Navy would be complete without some description of that great establishment in Washington which controlled the world-wide operations of our fleets. The terse business-like orders which cracked out daily from this nerve center to our far-flung ships at sea, indicated that we had a sharp, resourceful, and powerful organization watching over us. So although it will get me a little ahead of my story in places, I must take time out for a few pages to tell you about the Navy Department.

If you have any illusions which you wish to preserve about how Columbia rides safely through the storm, please put them away in a secure place before reading any more of this chapter. The Founding Fathers of this country must have foreseen the evolution of the Navy Department when they adopted the motto, "In God We Trust."

The loose, rambling hodgepodge of bureaus and offices which evolved from 150 years of U.S. history and presided over American sea power during World War II in a "temporary" World War I building, was one of the wonders of the modern world. The only thing that can be said in favor of it, from an organizational point of view, is that it hasn't lost a single war, so far.

Out in the middle of the Atlantic a word from the Navy Department was often like guidance direct from heaven. But when you went to Washington and saw the snarls of red tape, and the utter confusion in the halls from which this guidance came, you knew that the age of miracles had not yet passed. Every new Secretary of the Navy, a few months after he takes office, calls in a firm of management engineers to advise him on how to streamline the Navy Department's organization. These bright-eyed efficiency experts rub their hands in glee and chuckle to themselves the moment they start nosing around. "Boy, oh, boy," they say. "What a setup this is for us."

On paper the Navy Department is the most cockeyed organization that ever happened to grow up and survive. It is both horizontal and vertical at the same time. Overlapping responsibility and authority are normal, and everybody has his nose stuck into everybody else's business. Let's not say there is "dupl-c-t-on," because that is an obscene word these days. Say rather that there is "decentralization."

But after all, an organization is merely a means to an end. When the management experts finish their survey and bring in their report proposing to tear the Navy's old-fashioned house down and replace it with a modern streamlined edifice, we just drag out the history books. While the ghosts of John Paul Jones, Farragut, Dewey and Mahan look on approvingly, we thumb through the books and point out: "It says here the United States has fought in seven wars and won them all." So another voluminous report winds up in the growing file marked: "Plans for reorganizing the Navy Department."

The Navy has an excellent precedent for resisting change and sticking to the good old system. When unification broke out and we moved from our traditional ramshackle stronghold on Constitution Avenue and set up shop in the ultramodern Pentagon, we took a worse licking than we have ever gotten on the high seas! We should of stood in bed!

The years you spend pounding the ocean waves and fighting battles with the Japs are of no help whatever in preparing you for duty in Washington. To get along in Washington you've got to be a smooth operator, and should be able to talk a bird down out of a tree. I've known some officers whom you would follow to the gates of hell in a fight against a foreign enemy, but who couldn't protect themselves in the clinches on the shores of the Potomac. Captain John Crommelin is an outstanding example. Admiral Halsey took his Third Fleet right up the doorstep of Japan's national capital, but I notice that when he was on shore duty he gave the seat of our own government a wide berth.

Whenever I came to Washington to talk to the A.S.W. experts I always stopped in and made a bow to Admiral King. He was an Olympian figure—a real giant among the pygmies who scurried about in wartime Washington impersonating global strategists. Five minutes with Admiral King showed you why, despite the uproar and confusion on the lower levels in the military establishment, we won the Battle of the Atlantic and smashed the Japanese dream of Greater East Asia.

Behind his back Admiral King was known to the whole Navy as "Uncle Ernie," but he could be a Dutch uncle if the occasion demanded. It was rumored around Washington that he used to shave each morning with a blowtorch. I don't know how he ever got picked for a top-level Washington job, because he definitely was not the suave, glib type. He was a hard-boiled, two-fisted seafaring, flying and fighting man.

They say that his only comment when he was notified that he had been picked for the new job of "Cominch and C.N.O.," right after Pearl Harbor, was: "When the going gets tough, they always send for the sons of bitches." Scrupulously honest, Uncle Ernie denies having said this, but does admit, "I wish I had said it."

The public relations experts had trouble prying information out of Admiral King during the war. Once, when

93

the Air Force had been hogging all the headlines for some time, a high-powered reporter was sent around to interview Admiral King and get some favorable publicity for the Navy. After an unproductive interview, this scribe is alleged to have said, "If Admiral King had his way, the Navy would issue only one communiqué to cover the whole war. It would be released the day after the surrender and would read, 'We won.'"

I've known Admiral King for a long time, and I would rather not serve directly under him, except in battle. He is rather unreasonable about expecting other people to be as good as he is. He always impressed me as being made out of tool steel, and every time I saw him during the war, despite the backbreaking load of responsibility he carried, he looked younger and tougher than the time before.

I hope the Navy can always produce an Uncle Ernie to step in and run things when the fate of the country hangs in balance.

Whenever I went back to the *Guadalcanal* after a visit to Washington I always thanked my lucky star that I had escaped from the madhouse, and hoped that my luck would hold out. But eventually the Navy's system for rotation of duties caught up with me. After two and a half years of comparative peace and quiet in the Battle of the Atlantic they decided I was due for a rest, and gave me a desk in the boiler factory on Constitution Avenue.

There is no greater demotion for a naval officer than to go from the bridge of a combatant ship in wartime to a chair behind a desk ashore. At sea you are the monarch of as much ocean as you can survey. Ashore you become one of the horde of faceless bureaucrats at the beck and call of bigger bureaucrats. At sea, if you let out a growl, everybody falls flat on his face. Ashore if you say "boo," especially in Washington, the word goes around that you're getting too big for your britches. I suppose it is a good thing that naval officers are subjected to this periodic deflation of their ego; otherwise they might get mistaken ideas of their importance.

While I was trying to adjust myself to this demotion after leaving the *Guadalcanal,* my brother Phil had command of a destroyer which bombarded Corregidor from shotgun range when we recaptured Manila. Shortly after, he hit a mine which almost broke his ship's back. By expert seamanship he got her back to port under her own steam. To keep Philip in his proper place and prevent him from getting too cocky I sent him the following dispatch.

"Just because you've got a hole in your bottom, don't think you're a flower pot!"

When they finally corralled me from sea duty and tried to put shoes on me in Washington, I'm afraid I was somewhat balky at first. After breathing the salty air of the ocean for three years, I was inclined to gag on the atmosphere there.

Washington is a sort of a stratified place and the U.S. Government is organized in layers. Depending on the importance of your job you are either a high, a low, or an intermediate level character. Of course everyone in Washington is convinced that he belongs on the next higher level than the one he is currently on, and spends a great deal of his time trying to climb up there. Many of the people that I met seemed more concerned with convincing their bosses that they were up and coming individuals than they were with what went on in the theatres of war. But they chucked a good bluff at knowing what was going on because an efficient bureaucrat in any government department around that town is supposed to know all about everything and is never at a loss for a quick answer. Maybe the answer they come up with is wrong, but that doesn't matter too much, because the boys on the firing line can correct their blunders for them.

The Navy's bureaucrats were conspicuously the best of the lot in wartime Washington—I suppose because they *have* to spend at least half their time on sea duty, and so they usually have at least some firsthand idea as to the havoc their blunders can cause.

During my brief wartime duty in the Navy Department I sometimes helped to settle problems about which I knew nothing. But one of the many amazing things about the Navy Department organization is that a conference of officers, who individually know very little about the question at issue, can often come up with a remarkably sound solution to it. Maybe this is because everybody is peeking over the other fellow's shoulder so much. At any rate, there seems to be some subtle influence about the system that permeates the halls of the Navy Department and guides the bewildered seafarers when they need guidance.

Of course we often solved tough problems by simply hitting them with a sledge hammer; we took a "broad view" of the "overall picture." If the wildest guess that anyone could make was that we needed ten of a certain item in order to capture Iwo Jima, we would say, "Let's be on the safe side and provide a hundred." We weren't the only ones around Washington who did that. You will never persuade me that this wasn't our basic global strategy in World War II.

It was extravagant, of course. We *might* have won the war with a great deal less than we demanded. But the penalty for having too much was a big pile of surplus stuff on hand at the end of the war. The penalty for not having enough might be the loss of the war.

A lot of books have been written about the shrewd *military* strategy and tactics which led to victory in the various theatres. When I read some of the tripe that has been printed about the strategy and planning of World War II, I have a tendency to throw up. Future students of warfare will learn some very misleading lessons from these books if they fail to realize that the home front was the decisive theatre. The strategy of the production line dominated and made possible all the rest of the strategy. Those fifty Kaiser jeeps that slid down the building ways in Vancouver are an example of what I mean.

Our fantastic industrial production clinched the victory

before we ever put a soldier ashore. When our offensive in Europe and the Pacific finally got going we ran such a power play over tackle that it just couldn't be stopped.

We might have made all sorts of strategic and tactical blunders, but we would still have won by sheer momentum and the guts of our people on the firing lines. I wouldn't dream of saying that we did make any blunders. But our build-up of reserves provided insurance against making them. Had the Joint Chiefs of Staff decided to follow Churchill's scheme for hitting the "soft underbelly in the Balkans," I'm sure that our avalanche of armor, men, munitions, and planes would have swamped the enemy there just as it did in France.

The battles in which *military* strategy and tactics were decisive were those which we fought on a shoestring, such as Midawy, Guadalcanal and North Africa. Those battles were real tests of our tactical planning, our military forces, and their leadership, because there was very little in reserve behind the people on the firing line. We had to outsmart and outfight the enemy because we couldn't just bowl him over by sheer weight of numbers and equipment.

In the early part of the war, before our industrial plants got into high gear, certain strategic decisions were taken which had to be right. They were such things as deciding to lick Germany first, and not be panicked into premature action in the Pacific. Most of our two-ocean Navy was still on the building ways. We swallowed our pride and bided our time until we got it into the water.

All I know about those decisions is what I have read in the books written by Churchill, Eisenhower and the others who were in on their making. Fortunately, for succeeding generations of young Americans, one of the U.S. representatives at these powwows was that crusty old S.O.B., "Uncle Ernie."

During my stretch in the Navy Department I was Assistant Director of the Plans Division for naval aviation. This was obviously a very low-level job, but occasionally I did get up into the rarefied atmosphere on the global strategy level. I was an alternate member of the Logistics Committee of the Joint Chiefs of Staff, and whenever my principal could not attend the meetings I became one of the six voting members. This committee was a top-level agency of the Joint Chiefs of Staff and dealt with matters that made my head swim. At one meeting I helped decide how Germany would be divided up among the allied occupation forces when and if we conquered it. I say I helped, but all I did was vote "Yes" on the plan which the alleged experts in the J.C.S. system produced, and which we sent up for consideration by the chiefs themselves. Even so, I suppose that makes me partly responsible for the "botched" up mess that puts us out on a limb in Berlin and Vienna. I suspect that the decision to split Korea along the 38th Parallel was "processed" and "implemented" in the same manner.

For some time during my hitch in Washington I was overawed by the global planning hot shots who prepared studies for the Joint Chiefs of Staff, and figured that they personified military strategy and were infallible. I found out eventually that this was not strictly true in all respects.

Only once did I venture to take issue with any of the plans which these professional strategists produced. When our committee was scrutinizing the plans for the invasion of Japan I questioned the advisability of invading at all.

This was early in 1945 when the Japs were hanging over the ropes. I pointed out that the Jap Navy had been sunk, our submarines had driven the Jap merchant ships off the seas, and planes from the Fast Carrier Task Forces and the Strategic Air Force were making a shambles of the homeland. I asked: "Why go through the bloody ordeal of an amphibious landing when all we have to do is wait a little while and let nature takes its course?"

The General Staff boys looked at me as if I were a skunk at a lawn party. Our land-minded strategists simply didn't understand sea power and had no appreciation of what control of the sea can do in a fight against an island empire. England had eked out survival in two world wars by a narrow margin because she controlled the seas. But even though *we* had complete control of the seas around Japan our planners couldn't conceive of conquering a country without invading it.

I'm glad we didn't have to go through with that invasion plan. I'm pretty sure that, if we had, it would have succeeded by sheer massed power, and the people who planned it would now be able to point with pride to another brilliantly conceived and executed operation. But the cost would have been ghastly. The Japs, fighting a last ditch stand on their native shores, would have taken a terrific and wholly unnecessary toll of American lives.

So far as our military planning was concerned, the only objective we ever had in fighting the war was to win a military victory in the shortest possible time. The proposed invasion of Japan was an example of this type of planning. This lack of any postwar international strategy or broad policy objective was not the fault of the military. Under our system of government it is not the job of the military to make policy. It is their job to enforce and execute the policies decided on by the statesmen. If the statesmen can't give you any better strategic guidance than unconditional surrender as an objective, then perhaps "win the war and get it over with" is as good as any other overall military plan.

Maybe the establishment of the United Nations was supposed to fill the void in our postwar international policy. Looking back on it now, the Germans and Japs benefitted more by the cessation of hostilities than we did. We won the war in the sense that we escaped military defeat and enslavement by the Axis nations, but I don't know of much else that we got out of it. Twenty-three years after the end of World War I the victors in that war were on the brink of defeat in the next one. It's six years now since the end of the last war and the world is no better off now than it was six years after the end of the *first* "last" war. This is another demonstration that in the final analysis you don't win wars—you just avoid losing them.

Of course, military men, if they are so indiscreet as to say anything worth listening to these days, are supposed to preface their remarks with the pious hope that there will never be another war. That's like hoping that there will never be another hurricane. I don't say that wars are "inevitable," because every war that has ever been fought could have been avoided, if men had been willing to practice the high-sounding precepts which we all profess to believe. Man has been on this earth a long time, and one of the first recorded incidents of his sojourn here was a fight between two brothers in the Garden of Eden, in which one brother got killed. We have been following that example ever since. World War III started on VJ Day as a cold war. It began to warm up when the Russians blockaded Berlin and nearly reached the exploding point in Korea. Anyone who still thinks we can settle our differences with the Russians around a council table must still believe in Santa Claus.

I often hear it said that the Russian people, unlike their ruthless and cold-blooded leaders, are fundamentally good people. I agree. There is nothing wrong with the Russians that can't be cured by about thirty years of freedom and education. In the absence of those medicines more drastic remedies will probably be necessary.

When human nature changes to such an extent that you and I can live in peace with each other and don't need the cops to keep us from doing illegal things to each other, then it will be time to talk of the millennium when we can live in peace with the communists. No League of Nations or United Nations can bring permanent peace until the Major Powers are willing to surrender their sovereignty, and are not only willing but compelled to submit to unfavorable majority votes. I doubt if that Great Day is here yet, and until then we had better follow Teddy Roosevelt's advice: 'Speak softly, but carry a big stick."

We had the biggest stick the world has ever seen on VJ Day, but we threw it away. Before the gun barrels had time to cool the cry, "Bring the boys home," resounded through the land. In some overseas camps discipline collapsed and the cry was re-echoed by the "we wanna go home" crybabies.

Everybody thought that all international problems had been solved when the Japs came aboard the *Missouri* to sign on the dotted line. Both Germany and Japan surrendered unconditionally; Stalin was our great friend and ally; and the United Nations could produce papers signed by all major countries to prove that there could never be another war. The game was over, we had won the championship, and now the only thing that mattered was to get our domestic economy back to business as usual. We were all going to live happily ever after.

You can hardly blame the American people for swallowing this fairy story which nearly all of our statesmen endorsed. Some day we may develop statesmen who understand that war isn't like a baseball game in which the whole business is finished when one side or the other wins. Wars are fought for political purposes, and the accomplishment of those purposes doesn't begin until the war is over.

But the minute the shooting stopped in World War II blithely confident that whatever it was we had been fighting for was now secure, we demobilized our armed forces. "Demobilized," did I say? That isn't exactly the right word. It implies an orderly operation. We actually were panicked by the outbreak of peace, and the clamour at home and abroad. We ripped out the foundations and allowed our whole national defense structure to collapse!

In World War II, our Army, Air Force, and Navy smashed the most powerful military machine in history. Less than five years later the U.S. military forces were very nearly run out of Korea by a rabble of communist stooges!

On VJ Day the United States had the greatest Navy that ever sailed the seven seas. This Navy was a potential instrument of foreign policy which, if properly used could have helped to preserve the peace for future generations. It was a mobile and versatile force. The same ships which assisted in the capture of Saipan in 1942 could, if necessary, be used to bottle up the communist submarines on the other side of the world in 1962. They could perform missions ranging all the way from showing the flag in out-of-the-way places where our prestige needed strengthening, to Str-t-g-c-b-mb-rdm-nt* of an enemy capital. Our statesmen regarded this great Navy only an instrument of war, no longer needed.

Within a year most of our fleet was in moth balls. Within four years the Navy and Marine Corps were actually on trial for their lives before the Congress of the United States. If certain high officials had had their way naval aviation and the Marine Corps would have been abolished on the pretext of "trimming the fat off our armed forces." Of course, when we tried to eat our demobilization cake and have it, too, in Korea, we soon found out that the Navy and Marine Corps could still be of some use. Even the *Missouri* emerged from disgrace and hurled salvos of 16" shells into enemy troops 15,000 miles from that sand bar in Chesapeake Bay where she had made headlines only a few months before.

However, I have no doubt that after World War III, IV, V, and VI, we will as usual chase the will-o'-the-wisp of eternal peace and will put our armed forces through the wringer again as we always have. We will thus deprive ourselves of the one thing which might make the other ninety-five percent of the world's two billion people listen to us.

Despite the high level of American intelligence we seem incapable of recognizing the most fundamental fact of life on this earth today, namely that the world is still run by force.

But enough of this global philosophizing. At the time under discussion in this book I had other things to think about. Although I occasionally got into the high strategy at the Logistics Committee meeting, I usually worked at a

_____
* Copyrighted word which the Navy is not allowed to use.

more prosaic trade. One of my regular chores was to attend the daily conference in Admiral Horne's office each morning. I, a Captain, was the only aviator present among a dozen or so surface Admirals, and I came in for quite a lot of more or less good-natured ribbing whenever any of the foibles of aviators came up for discussion.

"Goddam-aviator" was still a hyphenated word in the Navy at this time, although the havoc wrought by Admiral Halsey's carrier task forces was beginning to build the aviator's position up to the point where we could refer condescendingly to our surface brethren as "the black shoe Navy."

At one of these conferences in Admiral Horne's office a new command organization for the Third Fleet was announced. Since the Third Fleet was built around aircraft carriers, the aviation Admirals drew all the plums in the new setup, and commanded the Carrier Task Forces. In many cases this placed comparatively junior flying Admirals over the heads of old-time Admirals, commanding battleships and cruiser divisions, who were far senior to the flying upstarts.

After some acrimonious discussion of the new setup, one old salt cocked his eye at me and said, "It's a funny Navy where they make the plebes senior to the first classmen."

I edged toward the door, got set to run, and replied, "As soon as the war is over, sir, and it's safe to do so, we will go back to the old system."

The day I turned over command of the *Guadalcanal* to Captain McCaffree, just before going to duty in Washington, I made a little speech to the crew, which apparently not a single one of them ever forgot. I said, "If I can ever be of help to any of you lads, don't hesitate to write to me and let me know." All of you boys must have thought I was going to Washington to be the dictator of the United States instead of only an assistant director of a division in the Navy Department. At any rate, while I was on duty in the Navy Department I received a constant stream of letters from them, asking me to get them transferred, promoted, or released from jail.

There was one letter which I'll never forget. It stated the essentials of a problem without going into any superfluous details. It said:

DEAR CAPTAIN:

Sir, I have been on shore duty at Pensacola for about seven months and was getting along fine. I have been promoted to second class and expect to make first class very soon. I remember our duty together on the *Can Do* very well and also remember what you said the day you left.

Sir, I am writing to you now to request your assistance. A situation has arisen here at Pensacola, and I would like very much indeed to be sent to sea duty.

Will you please see if you can arrange this?

Respectfully,

J. Doe

Of course, when a situation arises involving a seafaring man, obviously the only thing to do is to get him back to sea. I got him transferred.

I had a hard time getting housebroken to the gobbledegook which you have to use in official papers around the national Capitol. I had to learn how to use language in order to conceal thoughts rather than to express them. A properly written, high level, official paper must be vague, pompous, and verbose. There must be enough loose language in it so that each individual who reads it can interpret the paper as saying what he wants it to say. This gobbledegook is not a product of the much maligned military mind. We got it from the civilian side of the government, but the military have become pretty adept in its use.

One time I made a gesture of protest against this debasement of the language. At a cocktail party when Admiral Radford was Vice Chief of Naval Operations, Mrs. Radford and Mrs. Gallery were comparing notes. Mrs. Radford lived in Washington and had a garden which was badly in need of fertilizer. We lived in the country, had a couple of horses on the place, and therefore had a growing pile of fertilizer behind the barn. The two ladies preceeded to cook up a deal whereby I was to drive to work in my jeep the next morning, bring several bags of fertilizer along with me. Radford's gardener would come to my parking space at the Pentagon and pick it up.

I stubbornly refused to have any part of this deal, on the grounds that bringing sacks of horse manure in to the Pentagon would be exactly the same as carrying coal to Newcastle.

The most far-reaching decision in which I played a part during this tour of duty was in naming the U.S.S. *Franklin D. Roosevelt*. Early in 1945 our second Midway class carrier was nearly ready to launch, and she was slated to be called the *Coral Sea*. On the night that the stunning bulletin of the President's death interrupted the radio programs the thought occurred to me, as it did, I suppose to many others, that our next big ship should bear the name of the great man who understood sea power better than any other occupant of the White House except perhaps Roosevelt the first.

Next morning I went up to Vice Admiral Fitch, DCNO Air, and laid a memo on his desk suggesting that the name of the *Coral Sea* be changed to *F.D.R.* As Admiral Fitch read this memo his eyes began to sparkle, a grin reached from ear to ear, and when he finished reading he jumped up, banged his fist on the desk and said, "That's a hell of a good idea."

Within twenty-four hours President Truman had done the same thing. Then the plot began to thicken. The question of a sponsor for the *F.D.R.* came up. Of course, Mrs. Roosevelt was the first name that occurred to everybody—but there were complications.

It seems that the wife of a distinguished naval officer was slated to sponsor the *Coral Sea*. She had originally been picked to sponsor the *Bon Homme Richard* three years previously. Before the "Big Dick" was launched, the *Yorktown* got sunk, so we changed the name of the new ship to *Yorktown*. The lady who had sponsored the first *Yorktown* was still available, so it seemed appropriate to ask her to break the bottle over the stem of the new one. At that time we were building carriers in every back yard that had a view of salt water, so the lady who was to have sponsored the *B.H.R.* would not have long to wait for another one. She readily agreed to sponsor CV-38 for which no name had yet been selected.

But then Jimmy Doolittle made his raid on Tokyo, singlehanded and unaided by the Navy (except for the U.S.S. *Hornet* which took his short-legged bombers through Japanese controlled waters to within striking distance of Tokyo). After this great shot in the arm to U.S. morale F.D.R. made his famous crack about Doolittle's raid taking off from Shangri-La. This made so many headlines that the next carrier we launched just had to be called the *Shangri-La*. Obviously Mrs. Doolittle was the proper lady to sponsor a ship with that name.

The next carrier scheduled for launching was the still unnamed CV-38. So we named her the *Shangri-La*, and the secretary of the Navy again wrote the charming lady who had already been shuffled out of one christening, explaining this new development. He stated that a much bigger and better ship to be called the *Coral Sea* would be launched in 1945, and the Navy would deem it a great honor if she would sponsor that one.

The lady's reply to the Secretary was understandably cool this time. She was willing to do anything necessary to help in the war effort, but she was beginning to get fed up with the vacillating contemporaries of her husband who couldn't make up their minds.

Nobody thought of this previous history until the new name, *Franklin D. Roosevelt* had been officially announced

But then the Secretary of the Navy's aide remembered and his blood ran cold. For a day or so everybody in top-level circles around the Navy Department shook their heads and quoted the old saying: "Act in haste—repent at leisure."

Eventually their fears vanished into thin air. Mrs. Roosevelt didn't want to christen the *F.D.R.* only a month after her husband's death. So the lady who had been asked to sponsor the *B.H.R.* in 1942 finally broke the bottle over the stem of this great ship in 1945.

On a later tour of duty, after the war, I tried unsuccesfully to influence the naming of another ship. I took a dim view of the proposed name, U.S.S. *United States* for the so-called super carrier in 1948, later scuttled by the Hon. Louis Johnson. I could visualize headlines, "United States blows up"; ". . . is sunk"; or " . . . gets stuck in the mud."

I proposed in all seriousness that we give this ship a name that would exemplify the unification of the services; that would honor a great American; but which wouldn't be such a godsend to enemy propaganda agencies in case she came to grief. I proposed that we call her *Brig. General William G. Mitchell*. Everybody laughed when I sat down at the piano, and refused to treat the suggestion seriously.

But I've been getting ahead of my story. I still had three eventful cruises to make in the *Guadalcanal*, before I reported to Washington, so let's lash up our bag and hammock and get back to sea again where the Navy is more at home.

CHAPTER 6

DOWN TO THE SEAS

When you stamp the mud of the beach off your feet and put out to sea in a ship, you enter a cleaner and better part of the world. After the land drops out of sight astern, you can go up on deck and fill your lungs with clean salt air, uncontaminated by the stink of selfish intrigue and the dirty business that goes on ashore.

You search the sparkling water and the blue sky clear around the horizon without finding any indications of the sordid motives, hypocrisy, and deceit which surround you on shore.

At sea you know who your enemies are, and you can shoot at them on sight with high explosives. They can shoot at you too, of course, but they can't spread rumors behind your back or take advantage of your friendship to do you in.

In port a ship's company of a thousand men have interests that extend to every state in the union, touch every walk of life, and have ramifications ranging from the waterfront to the councils of the great. When they walk down the gangway to go ashore, it's every man for himself. But at sea all hands have just your own tight little community in the ship to think about; and all of you have a stake in the success of the ship.

When you shove off on a voyage in wartime everybody from the Captain on down to the lowest seaman puts his future into the pot. Every man aboard knows that whether you get back from that voyage safely or not may depend on him. All hands from a fine ship can wind up in the water simply because a grease monkey lets a main bearing run dry, a radio operator misses an urgent message, or a seaman lookout fails to see a torpedo track.

I used to tell my boys there was no such thing as an unimportant job on the ship, and that anybody who thought he had one could come up to the cabin and tell me about it. I said that if he could convince me I would immediately abolish that job, whatever it was, and give him something else to do.

To prove that point I once told my crew the story of the Captain of the Head in Iceland. In the Navy the "head" is, of course, the gentlemen's room, afloat or ashore. And Captain of the Head is the facetiously high-sounding title bestowed upon the lowly and unfortunate individual whose duty it is to swab out the bowls and keep everything shining and shipshape in that very-much-used compartment. When our PBY's in Iceland made their first kill I presented prize money to all members of the plane's crew at the movies that night, and then made a little speech proving that the Captain of the Head played an important part in making that kill.

The pitch was as follows: That flight took off an hour before sunrise, and the pilot got up, took a shower, shaved, and performed certain other important operations in the gentlemen's room before manning his plane and flying off into the wild blue yonder. If you have ever been associated with primitive washroom facilities such as we had in Iceland, you know that they are at best somewhat messy, and if the unfortunate menial whose duty it is to keep them as spic and span as possible falls down on the job, they can become very odious, indeed.

So if you were scheduled for an early flight and found the plumbing facilities in that condition, you might well say to yourself, "The hell with this, I'll wait a while." Then after you got your PBY in the air, were clear of the land, and had gotten squared away on the first leg of your patrol, you would go aft to perform the necessary business, using the reasonably civilized facilities of the Catalina airplane.

The point of all this is that opportunities to kill submarines are few and far between. You may fly several hundred hours without ever having a chance, and then suddenly without warning one is dumped in your lap and you have perhaps thirty seconds to cash in on it. If you are in the pilot's seat when this happens, with the bomb release within easy reach of your right hand, you may strike a blow for freedom and get yourself a medal. But if you are seated back aft with your pants down, when opportunity knocks, you won't become a hero on that flight.

So since this flight *had* sunk a submarine, this proved that the Captain of the Head had an important job, had done it well, and deserved part of the credit for the kill.

The whooping and hollering on the hangar deck when I finished telling my story indicated that my boys were still skeptical about the desirability of being Captain of the Head, and about the effect which that official might exert on the outcome of the war. But nobody came up to the cabin afterwards to try and convince me that his job wasn't important.

If an old-timer from sailing ship days were to come aboard a ship of the modern Navy, it wouldn't be long before he felt at home. For the first couple of days he would be amazed at the miracle of steam, and the array of mechanical gadgets that fill a ship today. But he would soon get his bearings, accept the new magic as commonplace, and would find that many things are still the same as they were in the old days.

The watches into which the day is divided, and the bells struck during the watch are the same today as they have been for centuries. The day at sea consists of six four-hour periods. It starts with the "midwatch," from midnight to 4:00 A.M. This is followed by the morning, forenoon, and afternoon watches, after which comes the "dog watch," from 4:00 to 8:00 P.M. This is usually split into two two-hour periods, to make an odd number of watches in a day, and thus prevent the same group of watch standers from being stuck with the same watch every day. The last watch of the day, from 8:00 P.M. to midnight, is known, with nautical perversity, as the "first" watch.

Bells are struck every half-hour and a new series of bells begins with every new watch; so eight is the greatest number of bells ever struck. Eight bells is, therefore, noon and midnight, 4:00 A.M. and P.M. and 8:00 A.M. and P.M. Although Columbus would still know what time it is by listening to our bells, it usually takes new recruits aboard a ship a little while to get on to the system.

One day I was completely flabbergasted to hear one of my salty young sailors tell his buddy, "I'll meet you ashore at eleven and a half bells!" (That rattling noise you just heard was caused by generations of old sailors turning over in their graves.)

The part of a modern ship where an old sailor would feel most at home and see the least change would be in the sailors' traditional hangout, the forecastle. The modern hawsepipes, anchor chains, stoppers, pelican hooks, and wild cats would require no explanation whatever. The old-timer would wonder why there were no capstan bars on the windlass, but would find the explanation if he went below into the doghouse and saw the anchor engines. Steam and electricity have now replaced all hands and the ship's cook at the capstan bars. The old-timer would be surprised at our newfangled patent anchors with their flat flukes and no stock, and probably would prefer the old-fashioned kind. So would I, if I were really in bad trouble and needed another anchor to keep me off a lee shore in a howling gale.

An old-fashioned anchor with its stock at right angles to the flukes is much more difficult to handle and stow than the new stockless type. But that stock will make the old-fashioned type dig into the bottom and hold, when the safety of your ship may depend on its holding, and when a patent anchor would simply drag through the mud and put you ashore.

Even the markings on the chain would be familiar to an old-timer, and he would be able to glance at the mooring shackle and see how to bend it on. Taking it full and by, I believe John Paul Jones' boatswain could come aboard a modern ship and in about half a day's time could learn to bring her to anchor and get her underway as easily as if he were still aboard the old *Bon Homme Richard*.

Believe it or not, we had an ex-warrant machinist running our forecastle—Lieutenant Marty Lince. Marty had plenty of naval experience, but it was all in engine rooms. However, he had been with me up in Iceland for a year and a half, and I knew that he was one of those sailormen who could set taut and hoist away with any job you gave him.

I grant you that it was wasting talent to take a man with his engineering experience and put him up on the forecastle to learn a new trade in the middle of a war. The I.B.M. machines in the Bureau of Personnel in Washington must have slipped a cog, or maybe somebody pushed the wrong button, but anyway they ordered Lince to the *Guadalcanal* when we already had Earl Trosino for Chief Engineer. The only spot open for Marty was First Lieutenant and Damage Control Officer.

So, he had to forget about boilers, pumps, and turbines and learn about anchors, towlines, bulkhead shores, and fire fighting. He did it so well that he eventually became the last Commanding Officer of the *Guadalcanal,* and put her in moth balls after the war.

The leadsman in the chains would also be familiar to an old-timer, although I fear that the leadsman will not be there much longer. The fathometer, a mechanical gadget in the chart house, has already rendered him obsolete. This modern scientific marvel bounces echoes off the bottom of the sea and determines the depth of water by measuring the time interval between the outgoing and returning signals. However, the leadsman hasn't found out about this yet because a Navy Regulation of ancient vintage is still on the books, requiring him to be in the chains whenever a ship is in shallow water on soundings.

If a ship were unlucky enough to run aground without a leadsman in the chains, the skipper would have two strikes on him before any evidence was heard by the court-martial; so we still heave the lead despite the fathometer. The leadsman in a high speed ship today has to work a lot faster than his predecessors in sailing vessels. His lead line is still marked, as of old, by bits of colored rags and pieces of leather, and he uses the time-honored phraseology to report the depth of water he finds. That is, he uses it if he knows it. I once heard a youngster, who had a throwing arm like Joe DiMaggio, sing out, after a tremendous heave, "Near the red rag," when what he meant was, "By the deep six."

A certain number of the daily routine reports have survived from the early days of sail and have been handed down by successive generations of sailors to the modern Navy. The first, occurring during the forenoon watch, concerns the condition of the magazines. Around four bells of the forenoon watch, the gunner approaches the Captain on the bridge, salutes, hands him a small piece of paper and says, "Magazine'spowdersampleinspectedtemperaturesnormal." The Captain returns his salute, replies, "Very well," and then goes over to the rail and puts in several minutes of deep study over the piece of paper, which simply sets forth the maximum and minimum temperatures of the magazines. Then he folds it up into a small wad, and sees how far he can flip it out from the side of the ship, and resumes his regular station on the bridge, ready for the next emergency that arises.

At noon the quartermaster reports, "Twelve o'clock, chronometers wound," and delivers the navigator's report of the ship's position and run since noon of the previous day. There is quite a gay display of bunting from all yardarms in the task group as each ship signals its noon position. Any ship which lags behind the others in making this signal is immediately suspected of "gun decking" her navigation by reading and averaging the other ships' signals.

The term "gun deck" sight is applied to a calculation which is worked out, knowing the ship's position in advance and working backward from this known position to calculate what the sun's altitude would have been had it actually been measured with a sextant. This seemingly futile form of navigation has great practical value to lazy midshipmen on their summer cruises, and the fact that you can't see the sun or the stars from the gun deck does not affect its accuracy, provided you have had a good peek at the navigator's work sheet or at the other ships' noon signals.

The navigator of the flagship is always quite pleased and satisfied with himself when the average of the noon signals confirms his own figures. When they do not, he shakes his head and mutters about "those clumsy destroyer sailors" who "don't know how to read a sextant."

The last report of the day is at eight bells in the evening. The O.O.D.'s messenger comes down to the cabin and says, "The O.O.D. reports eight o'clock, eight o'clock lights and galley fires out, prisoners secure." That is, perhaps once out of a hundred times a messenger succeeds in remembering all this. Most of the time all the messengers had to say by the time they got to my cabin was, "Sir, it's eight o'clock."

You run into strange things at sea. Of course, sailors soon get accustomed to whales, blackfish, porpoises, and "Mother Carey's chickens." The sharp, unmistakable line of demarcation between the deep blue of the Gulf Stream and the Atlantic's normal sickly green, becomes a commonplace fact of life to the deck force. The engineers on watch below do not have to see this line to know when you cross it. They watch the circulating pumps on the main condensers for a sudden change in the injection temperature.

During a battle of the Atlantic, odd bits of wreckage go floating by. One day far at sea we met a large steel tank, about as big as a locomotive, sailing along like a cork;

we had some good target practice sinking it. One night we had an exciting four-hour duel of wits with a disappearing radar blip, that kept bobbing up again. We were certain we had a sub that time but when the sun rose it showed our "enemy" was a small, empty, metal dory from a ship sunk several months before. Another night a tiny light bobbing around in the middle of the Atlantic aroused alarm at first, and then curiosity. Finally, after circling warily a couple of times, we went to a lot of trouble to fish an aviator's life jacket out of the ocean with a small flashlight attached. The battery on this jacket was only good for twenty-four hours and was still burning brightly, but we never solved the riddle of how it got there.

The most unusual phenomenon we ever encountered was a swarm of butterflies, so help me, halfway between Bermuda and Norfolk. I sent for Bikkers, our navigator, and icily inquired as to how sure he was of his position. He indignantly asserted that he was positive of it, until I pointed to those butterflies fluttering around on the flight deck. The Dutchman disappeared abruptly into the chart house, emerged again a few minutes later shaking his head, vehemently stated, "Dose gottam butterflies are lost, Cap'n; not us."

By custom, dating back to the time of Noah, the captain lives alone aboard ship, but he gets lots of service. My cabin steward, Evangelista, was a prewar Navy veteran of fifteen years' service. He saw plenty of action in the Pacific before he came to us, and had been sunk in the U.S.S. *Helena*. His main ambition in life was to complete his twenty years in the Navy and retire to his home in the Philippines after we recaptured them. He and the mess boys used to inspect my plate carefully when I finished each course of dinner, and I could often overhear conversations from the pantry, "He don't like de spinach." "He's eat op hall de meat." Whenever we had something special for dessert the usual chatter in the pantry would stop as soon as the plate was placed on the table. I knew that three pairs of eyes were peeking through the curtains behind me, anxiously waiting to see whether I ate the dessert or pushed it aside. This puts you in a tough spot. When he is fighting a battle of the Atlantic, the skipper's stomach is often full of those butterflies that we had on the flight deck, and he doesn't want dessert. But it seemed a shame to disappoint those eager eyes in the pantry.

Sometimes I got more service from Evangelista and the boys than I wanted. I could never take my coat off for a minute without having one of the boys grab it off the back of the chair, where I usually hung it, put it on a coat hanger, and stuff it into the locker in the clothes closet. That meant that if the O.O.D. should suddenly yell down the voice tube that we had just sighted the *Tirpitz,* I had to lose a precious minute fumbling around to find my coat or else go into what might be a historic battle in my shirtsleeves.

Sailors sometimes find queer ways of amusing themselves. One day a mess boy engaged in a perfectly innocent pastime had me thinking for a few moments that I was beginning to crack up and have hallucinations. On a bright sunshiny afternoon we were cruising downwind at such speed that the relative wind past the ship was almost zero. I was standing off on a wing of the bridge daydreaming when suddenly I thought I saw a brilliantly colored pink soap bubble about four inches in diameter go floating past me about ten feet way.

I snapped out of my dreams with a start, and gaped at this apparition drifting out of sight astern. As it disappeared, I thought fast, and decided that it probably just wasn't so. After all, I had been up all night, and had been in a pretty deep reverie when the thing appeared, so maybe it was best to just ignore it. I had just finished rationalizing the event when a blue and a green bubble came floating by. This time there could be no doubt whatever about what I thought I saw——they were brilliantly colored soap bubbles!

So I rapidly revised my estimate of the situation to

allow for the fact that apparently I actually was seeing soap bubbles. This was improbable—but not impossible. However, I had to make sure of it and find out where they were coming from before saying anything about it.

A careful check for the next few minutes showed that the bubbles were coming from under the overhang of the flight deck near my cabin. I hurried down to the cabin, ostensibly to get a clean handkerchief, but actually to check up on those bubbles.

To my great relief I found one of my mess boys with his head stuck out the port, blowing colored soap bubbles over the side.

I had to make this personal check before calling the phenomenon to the attention of anyone else on the bridge. If I had asked the Officer of the Deck to verify it for me, just as sure as fate my mess boy would have picked that exact moment to quit blowing bubbles. Before long word would have gotten all over the ship, "The Captain thinks he is seeing pink soap bubbles."

People have been saying since before Columbus' time that a sailor has a wife in every port. I'm afraid that if you ask anyone who served in the *Guadalcanal* about this they may think of me, and affirm emphatically that this is still true; but if you give me time enough I can explain everything.

In the first place, I have two brothers in the regular Navy who are a few years younger than I am. One of the first ports that we stopped in, on our shakedown cruise, was San Diego, and there I found Mrs. Bill Gallery. Bill, one of the early settlers on Guadalcanal, was out in the South Pacific at that time around New Guinea, blazing a trail for the later fabulous operations of the Black Cats. Naturally I had Mrs. Bill out aboard ship for dinner, introduced her to everybody in the wardroom as "Mrs. Gallery," and took her to the movies on the hangar deck. Mrs. Bill is worth a second look in any company, and all hands took a good gander and approved.

At our next port of call Mrs. *Phil* Gallery came aboard

and was duly introduced. She was about the same size and shape as the first Mrs. G. and was also able to hold her own in any company—but was definitely not the same one. I didn't go into any details in introducing her, because, after all, why the hell should the skipper have to come up with a long-winded explanation every time he brings a good-looking gal aboard?

Not long after this we stopped in a port where Zasu Pitts, of movie fame, was appearing in a stage play. Zasu at one time was married to Tom Gallery, a cousin of mine, and their beautiful eighteen-year-old daughter was touring with her. They both came out to the ship, and so all the officers met Miss Gallery and her mother. By this time people were beginning to wonder; but in the middle of World War II there is no use taking time out to go into a lot of family history, so I just let it go at that.

Finally the one and only authentic Mrs. D. V. Gallery came aboard when we got to Norfolk. She, likewise, is no crow; in fact, some unkind souls sometimes wonder how a broken-down seafaring man like me was ever able to pull the wool over the eyes of such a snappy number as Mrs. G. I noted a distinct atmosphere of skepticism when I again appeared in the wardroom and introduced "Mrs. Gallery." I could almost *hear* everybody saying mentally, "Oh, yeah?"

I mentioned earlier that each ship is different from every other ship, and naturally every Captain thinks that *his* ship is unique. One morning I found out right from the horse's mouth that our ship was just the same as the rest of them.

Two colored mess boys were sitting on deck outside the cabin during the morning watch shining a large collection of officer's shoes, and philosophizing about life in the Navy. One was a new recruit just out of the cotton fields and the other an old salt from the prewar Navy. The old-timer was explaining to the newcomer about life at sea, and I overheard the following gem of naval lore:

"Sebben years in de Navy shinin' shoes. . . . Shine de white shoes; shine de black shoes; shine de aviators' brown shoes. . . . De battleships are all de same as de carriers, 'cep'n you don' have so many brown shoes."

Old-timers would have little difficulty in understanding the language which we use at sea today. Much of it goes back to the early days, and they would pick up the meaning of the new, unfamiliar terms at least as quickly as an Iowa farm boy learns that when the word is passed for the lee helmsman to lay up to the bridge on the double, it means for the makey-learn steersman to repair to the wheelhouse expeditiously. The old-timer would know what the binnacle list, scuttle butt, and smoking lamp mean, although he would search in vain for this familiar lamp when the word is passed that it is lighted. The galley smoke pipe is still known as the "Charley Noble," although why I don't know, and the gentlemen's room is still the "head." If the old-timer heard the word passed, "Lay below all chain tierers," he would know the ship was about to heave in the anchor and get underway. The terms port and starboard, forward and aft, amidships and athwartships, below and aloft, deck, bulkhead and overhead would all be familiar to him. Ditty boxes and hammocks have disappeared only recently from our ships; but the boatswain's mate still blows his pipe and passes the word as he did in the old days, although the word is now carried to the far parts of the ship by squawk boxes rather than by the capacity of the boatswain's lungs and the alertness of his mates.

There is one word which makes everyone's blood run cold when it rings through a ship. The cry, "Man overboard!" on a dark night strikes a chill into every heart in the ship, but it hits the skipper harder than anyone else. He knows that what he does in the next five minutes will determine whether his man is recovered or lost.

We heard the cry once on the *Guadalcanal* early in our career, when a green sea lifted one of our lookouts out of his station at the forward end of the flight deck and carried him overboard.

I did everything I could think of that night, but it wasn't good enough. I couldn't find our man. Everyone in the ship knows that looking for a man in the water on a black night with a rough sea running is practically hopeless, and that a man can only survive for about ten minutes at most in near-freezing water, but, even so, you hate yourself when you give the order to resume course and leave the spot. It's like abandoning the search for a lost child.

Modern lookouts use the traditional cry of "Sail ho" when they first sight an object at sea.

The O.O.D. replies to "Sail ho" with the query, "Where away?"

The lookout states the bearing in nautical terms such as, "Three points abaft the starboard beam."

The O.O.D. then inquires, "Can you make her out?"

The lookout replies with a description of whatever it is he sees, as, for instance, "An hermaphrodite brig with a one-eyed Chinese cook."

This time-honored ritual should be memorized by lookouts, the same as altar boys learn the Mass ritual. Newcomers attempting to be salty sometimes betray their ignorance by singing out, "Ship ahoy," when the object sighted is way beyond hailing distance and has not yet been identified.

Ships meeting at sea, except in wartime, are much more civil to each other than strangers meeting ashore. At the very least they always exchange international call signs so that they can log each other's names. On request they will state their port of departure, destination, and weather encountered which may be of interest.

The pertinent items of information on a passing ship are about the same as those for a person. You want to know her name, nationality, occupation, age, and size. A good seaman always inspects the top hamper of passing ships and comments on any Irish pennants or other un-seamanlike features which he notes.

A ship's sea manners will sometimes tell you a lot about her skipper. Some merchantmen make it a practice, if they are going to pass within two miles of you, to maneuver so as to place you on their port bow. They do this on the theory that in any lawsuit over a collision in which a ship is rammed on her port side the burden of proof will be on the other vessel. Sometimes these sea lawyers flagrantly violate the rules of the road in order to put you on their port hand. I don't care to meet that kind of skipper either at sea or ashore.

Maritime law is the oldest code of law in the world. Under this code a ship is endowed with a personality. You bring suit against the ship herself, not her owners, in an admiralty court. The U.S. Marshal arrests the ship when she is libeled after an accident. The owners defend the ship in court, and, if you are awarded damages, they can bail her out and pay the damages; otherwise the ship is sold to meet the claims against her. If a little spit kit owned by a very wealthy company rams and sinks your ten-million-dollar ship, the admiralty court can pay you off in full by awarding you a free and clear title to the spit kit.

A time-honored custom of the sea is that of merchant ships dipping their colors when they meet men-of-war, a custom which originated back in the days of Drake. It is a very humiliating experience for the skipper of a man-of-war nowadays to have a merchantman dip to him and find his ship unready to answer this courtesy smartly. We were very punctilious about this on the *Guadalcanal,* but just when I thought we had that little item of ship's routine well mastered, it got us into a conspicuous and unthinkable breach of naval etiquette.

Of course, a man-of-war *never* dips her colors first; she merely returns dips. The only time a ship of war lowers her colors to another is in token of surrender, a possibility

121

which we had ruled out for the *Guadalcanal* in my commissioning address.

As we entered the Virginia Capes for the first time, we had a new lad standing by the colors to answer dips from merchant ships. Jus inside the Capes we met the giant carrier *Essex* sailing for Tokyo under the command of my good friend Tommy Sprague. As this latest addition to our carrier task forces boiled past us on her way to the war we all thrilled with pride, but felt rather small and insignificant ourselves. My lad at the halyards back aft evidently was overawed by the *Essex* too, because he promptly dipped his colors, precipitating an explosion on our bridge which nearly blew him overboard.

"Side boys" are an old seagoing institution which still survives. Side boys simply stand on each side of the gangway platform and salute when visiting officers or dignitaries come aboard, the number of boys in attendance being proportional to the rank and importance of the visitor.

Modern sailors have some interesting theories about the origin of this universal naval custom. One is that in sailing ship days, when visitors came aboard from passing ships at sea, they were usually hoisted aboard in a boatswain's chair, and the side boys manned the whip and did the hoisting. Since high-ranking officers were better fed and usually more portly than junior officers, the number of hands required to do the hoisting would increase with the hoistee's rank. This theory is partially confirmed by the fact that the boatswain still "pipes" important visitors over the side, and of course a boatswain with his pipe would supervise every hoisting operation whether it involved a dinghy or an ambassador.

Another theory is that the side boys' job was to help rum-laden visitors to get up the gangway, and that the higher the rank, the drunker they were. Since an Admiral rates eight side boys, the VIP's really must have been blotto in the old days, according to this theory.

Some people think that many old customs such as side

boys are of no practical value and should be abolished. That depends on what you mean by "practical." Churches find rituals and ceremonies to be of practical value. So do courts, legislative bodies, and fraternal organizations. They remind the participants of the traditions, philosophy, and authority of the organization using them.

The Navy has its rituals too—change of command ceremonies, gun salutes, morning and evening colors, passing honors for ships, hand salutes to the quarterdeck, and side boys. They were observed on the *Constitution,* the *Monitor,* and the *Oregon.* If you go aboard an aircraft carrier in Tokyo Bay, a cruiser in the Gulf of Aden, or a battleship in Chesapeake Bay, you will find them all observed in exactly the same manner today. This very sameness reminds us that it is all one Navy and that, if proper authority hoists the signal flags "Turn Pennant—Nine Flag," both the *Missouri* and LST # So-and-So will recognize the flags, and will make a ninety-degree right turn when the signal is executed by hauling it down.

These naval rituals link the present day Navy with the Continental Navy of John Paul Jones, They remind the young seaman of today, fresh from the cornfields, that he's serving in the same Navy which gave birth to the phrases, "Don't give up the ship," and "I have not yet begun to fight."

Are such things of any *practical* value? They support the heroic traditions dating back to the days of sail which inspire men to do things above and beyond the call of duty. I think they are just as "practical" as the proximity fuse.

One of the Captain's routine jobs is that of inspecting his ship and crew periodically. Once a week the Captain is supposed to line the crew up and inspect their uniforms and personal appearance, and to go around the ship and inspect the compartments for cleanliness. In the battle ship Navy in which I served my apprenticeship back in the 1920's, this Saturday inspection was quite a ceremony. Some of the old-time skippers used to pride themselves on their eagle eye which could detect non-regulation, tailor-made suits of blues further than they could identify a light on a dark night, and on their uncanny ability to find the dark corners and out-of-the-way places where the last bits of dirt were swept in cleaning up for the weekly ritual. In my younger days I used to think that a Captain should have more important matters on his mind, and that, if the old martinets had devoted as much thought to the important things as they did to the minor details, we would have had better ships.

My inspections were rather ragtime in some respects. I never paid much attention to such things as non-regulation haircuts, but I used to require each division officer to name every man in his division as we passed down the ranks, and asked him to tell me something about two or three men selected at random. This innovation made the division officers sweat, at first, but also made them get acquainted with their men.

However, at one time I decided that maybe the old-timers were not entirely wrong after all. Cleanliness and order have always been traditional aboard ship. In peacetime a smart ship is always a clean ship, and a dirty ship is usually a slack one. There is little excuse for not keeping things shipshape even in wartime, although some people got careless about this, and I was one of them.

I didn't realize just how slack we had gotten until one day on the way to the bridge I saw an orange peel lying under the Captain's ladder, and remembered that the peel had been there the day before. I was about to tell my orderly to heave it overboard when I thought, "Any real salty sailorman would do it without being told." I decided to wait and see how many days that orange peel stayed there. I'll bet it would be there yet if I hadn't given up after a week, torn between duty, curiosity and stubbornness every time I went up or down that ladder. As a sort of penance for letting the ship get into such a lubberly condition, I finally tossed it overboard myself.

That night at the movies I raised quite a stink about

that orange peel. As I talked to the crew it grew from a tiny dunghill to a mountain of monstrous proportions, and our proud little ship became a honey barge. We added a new article to the ship's regulations that night: "The *Guadalcanal* will be a smart, seamanlike ship." We never went in for spit and polish, but from then on we had a ship that a regular Navy sailor didn't have to be ashamed of.

In the old days the Captain used to pass judgment on offenders and assign punishment by holding a public hearing on deck at the foot of the mainmast. We still speak of bringing offenders "up to the mast," although mast is now held in any convenient public place such as the quarterdeck, because many modern ships actually have no mast, properly speaking. One time a boatswain's mate on the *Guadalcanal* who didn't understand the origin of this term passed the word on the loudspeakers, "Now the Captain will hold Mass in ten minutes." I immediately sent the orderly to Father Weldon to assure him that I had no intention whatever of committing such a sacrilegious irregularity. The Navy has advanced a long way since the days when the Captain could award floggings and keelhaulings at mast—but it hasn't come that far.

It was by no means unusual for me to come out of my emergency cabin unexpectedly during the small hours of the night and find my orderly asleep in his chair. Sleeping on watch is a serious offense for which you can be given *stiff* punishment. According to the book, "Anyone who sleeps upon his watch may be punished with death."

So a sleeping orderly presents the skipper with a dilemma. If he takes any notice whatever of the offense he must take serious action. You can't bring a man up to the mast for sleeping on watch and then merely slap him on the wrist. But these orderlies were growing kids who certainly didn't mean to sleep and who were ready to die, if necessary, in defense of their country.

It's no good to reach out and shake the boy by the

shoulder, because, if you do that, he knows it is your duty to do a lot more; and you can't let him sleep.

The solution to this problem was to anchor the orderly's chair in such a position that I couldn't come out of my cabin while he was seated without tramping on his toes and stumbling over his shins. If the orderly was awake he would, of course, get up on his feet as soon as he heard the door knob turn. If he was asleep I could crack his shins and apologize to him for my clumsiness while he was waking up, apparently not noticing his crime.

Keeping the night watches under a clear sky at sea is good for your soul. On a darkened bridge at night the full grandeur of the heavens soaks into you as it never can on shore. When you watch the majestic procession of the constellations across the zenith you can't help thinking of the millions of light years that separate us from the stars, of how long they have been there, of their uncountable numbers, and of their vast bulk dwarfing our earth to insignificance. It helps you to put this puny planet of ours and its wars in proper perspective.

It does a lot more than that. It does more than a sermon in St. Patrick's Cathedral to make you *know* beyond possibility of doubt that there is an omnipotent and all-wise God, and that the only reason you were born into this world was to serve Him, and be happy forever with Him after you die.

Look up at Orion, the greatest constellation in our northern sky. My mother taught me to recognize him when I was a kid seven years old. Orion hasn't changed much in the meantime. But the forty trips that you have made around the sun on this earth since then have changed you. Orion will make his nocturnal sweep across the sky for many, many more years. You wonder if he will notice it when you no longer look up and nod at him from this planet.

You gaze at Polaris, the hub of our Universe. He impartially shows true North to all seafaring and flying men, whether they be Americans, Russians, Britons, Nazis or Japs. You ask Polaris, "Don't you know there's a war on?" Polaris simply goes right on announcing, "Here is North."

There is Jupiter. In the quartermaster's glass you can see four of his moons nearly always in perfect line. He has eleven moons; but you need an astronomer's telescope to see them all. They circle around their parent very nimbly, sometimes disappearing behind him, and sometimes throwing their shadows on his disc as they pass in front.

Not so very long ago Galileo built a telescope and became the first man to gaze at this working model of our solar system. Until that moment the wisest men on earth still believed that the earth was the center of the Universe, and the sky revolved around us. Galileo's first glimpse of Jupiter's moons lifted the scales which had clouded men's eyes for thousands of years. Only four hundred years ago one look through a telescope like this one on the bridge turned man's concept of the Universe inside out. Tonight, you and I and the O.O.D.'s messenger glance at this marvel when we have nothing else to do, and turn away from it to listen to the ten o'clock news broadcast of things that will be forgotten next week.

There are Sirius, Aldebaran, the Pleiades, and Cassiopeia. In all the wars of the world so far these stars have been neutral. Now man is plotting to latch on to their light with navigating devices for guided missiles so that we can make the stars help us kill each other in the next war. If man ever succeeds in this sacrilegious plot the One who keeps the stars in their appointed places should destroy this evil world of ours.

But even if He should destroy it with an atomic blast and scatter the ashes from here to Polaris, like dust before a cosmic wind, the rest of the stars would still continue in their appointed revolutions and rotations undisturbed. Our planet is so puny that even our nearest neighbors in the solar system would never know the difference.

Many of our present-day wise men claim that in the

past four hundred years they have learned the answers to any questions you can ask about the whys and where-fores of Creation. They have determined the velocity of light even though the sixth decimal place is uncertain. They know that the diameter of the great star, "Beetle-juice," as the quartermasters call it, exceeds that of the earth's path around the sun. They know that the ponder-ous masses of the stars, their orbits, and their velocities through the heavens are all governed by a great code of law, and they can quote and explain this code in great detail until you ask them, "Whence came these laws?" Then some of these men who claim to be wise tell you that the whole business got started by chance, without any rhyme, reason, or Cause. Maybe you can believe this if you are sitting in a lecture hall ashore—but not when you look up from a ship on the open sea.

These same stars have watched everything that ever happened on this earth, and have seen all history in the making. Will the Battle of the Atlantic—or even World War II be mentioned in the logbook of the Universe? Why should they be?

The only event of any cosmic significance that ever happened on earth took place two thousand years ago. At that time Man crucified his Saviour, and we have been robbing and murdering each other ever since. Whether the next war lasts five years or fifty, whether we win or lose, this earth will look exactly the same to an observer on Orion as it has always looked.

The heavenly logbook might well sum up the past two thousand years of earth's existence with the usual entry for an uneventful watch: "As before, no remarks."

The celestial spheres roll on, and toward the end of the midwatch the early light of dawn appearing in the eastern sky tells the watch that in another hour Nature's greatest daily miracle, the sunrise, will be performed. Soon there will be another day on earth during which you can do good or evil. How many more sunrises must there be before we beat our swords into plowshares, and spend our time on this earth as our Creator wants us to?

All this philosophizing during the night doesn't change the fact that you are scouring the ocean beneath those eternal stars with planes bent on killing a U-boat, which will kill you if she gets a chance. But it does make you listen a little more attentively when Father Weldon comes up to the bridge after sunrise to say the morning prayer.

If you are watching the sea horizon at exactly the right spot on a clear day at sunrise or sunset you will see the "green flash," a phenomenon that landsmen are seldom privileged to witness. For the first or last few seconds as the upper rim of the sun peeks over the horizon its color changes quite suddenly to a brilliant green. There is a whole chapter in the physics books explaining this, but all you really have to say, if people try to pin you down about it, is that it's due to the refraction of light, and the sequence of colors in the spectrum. We always watched for this both at sunrise and at sunset, and my young sailors were greatly pleased with this addition to their seafaring lore.

After I explained a little trick to the boys, those who were in the air at dawn often saw the sunrise twice on the same day. If you are up at ten thousand feet your horizon is 115 miles away, but down at one hundred feet it is only eleven miles distant. The sun rises above the 115-mile horizon about seven minutes before it gets above the eleven mile one. So on a clear morning you can watch the sunrise once from ten thousand feet, and then dive rapidly down to one hundred feet, meantime watching it "set" in the east, and then after circling there for a few minutes at one hundred feet you see it rise again. This little experiment proves convincingly that the world is round and gives you material for astounding your friends, and perhaps collecting a few bets from skeptics who won't believe your "twice on the same day" story.

Of course, now that we have jet airplanes which can go west faster than the sun you can do this in reverse by chasing the sun after it has set, overhauling it, and thus bringing it up over the horizon again and seeing it *set* twice in one day.

Despite the fact that an old-timer soon learns to feel at home in a modern ship, many far-reaching changes have occurred in the structure and equipment of ships since the days of sail. There have been far-reaching changes in the character of the crew, too. Perhaps our lads today are not as tough in some respects as the old-timers, but they are certainly more intelligent, better educated, and at least as brave.

There is a well-known old saying: "Wooden ships with iron men are better than iron ships with wooden men." I won't dispute this, but the fact that we have iron ships today doesn't mean that we have wooden men. I found out that my lads were made of the same stuff as the ship.

Old-timers are fond of comparing the present-day Navy with the Navy of their heyday, shaking their heads sadly and saying, "The Navy ain't what it used to be." I'll probably do it myself some day. But if you ask now, I'll tell you that each new generation of American sailors is better than the one before it. Maybe they don't swear quite so saltily; maybe they don't start as many waterfront brawls or drink up as much alcohol from compasses. But put them up against the enemy in battle and they perform just as well as the old-timers did.

Parents are worrying now about the drafting of eighteen-year-olds, because they fear the lads taken away from home at this age may be corrupted by military service.

A hitch in the Navy has never been the basic cause that ruined any lad. What the Navy *will* do is to bring out and emphasize whatever the lad has in him. If a boy has had proper home training for eighteen years he will come out of the Navy at least as good as when he went into it—and maybe better. If he hasn't had proper home training he may come out a lot worse. But another year or two of improper home training wouldn't help those lads anyway. All except the really bad eggs are made better

130

citizens with a knowledge of discipline and respect for constituted authority which cannot be acquired on a college campus.

CHAPTER 7

A LOOK UNDER THE HOOD

The old-timer would be completely lost in the engine room of a modern ship, but if by any chance you think there is no romance left in a marine steam engineering plant, read "McAndrew's Hymn" by Kipling:

Lord, Thou hast made this world below the shadow of
   a dream,
An', taught by time, I tak' it so—excepting always
   Steam.
From coupler-flange to spindle-guide I see Thy Hand,
   O God—
Predestination in the stride o' yon connectin'-rod. . . .

The uninitiated, upon entering an engine room, is greeted by a meaningless medley of mechanical noises. To an engineer it is an orderly symphony of sounds, each having its own particular meaning. If the sound changes, a good engineer can go right to the source as quickly as Toscanini can put his finger on an erring fiddler. Each revolution of the main shaft produces a beat which sets the tempo for the whole tune. The Chief can tell pretty closely how many turns you are making by listening to this beat without even looking at the revolution counters.

I spent my first three years after graduation from the Academy in engineering duty in battleships, cruisers, and destroyers, and I still know my way around in an engine room. In fact, whenever I get into one, I always manage to ask a few questions designed not so much to elicit information, as to show off the fact that I know what it's all about.

It's a good thing for the skipper to know something about what goes on down below, although many chief engineers will tell you it's not always an unmixed blessing from their point of view. It requires the chief to be a lot more specific than would be necessary otherwise when he comes up to the bridge to tell the skipper he has got to slow down.

I cut my eyeteeth as an engineer when I was a midshipman in the *Maine,* a battleship with triple-expansion reciprocating steam engines and coal-burning boilers. (Let me make it clear that this was *not* the *Maine* that got blown up in Havana. I wasn't even born until several years after that.) But I heaved many a shovelful of coal into those boilers of the second *Maine,* learned how to make mulligan stew in a coal shovel stuck into the fire box; and nearly broke my back filling coal bags and trimming bunkers whenever we coaled ship.

Present-day sailors don't know how lucky they are to escape the periodic nightmare of coaling. When that little chore was completed all hands and the ship's cook looked like black-faced minstrels, and there was a thick layer of coal dust all over every compartment in the ship. We used to coal from both sides with the port watch competing against the starboard. The idea was to take the coal aboard so much faster on your side than they did on the other that you would list the ship over your way. Whichever side first got a two-degree list on the ship won an extra liberty. I remember we had a hell of a fight on the *Maine* once when we found out that a crooked freshwater king had taken a bribe of twenty bucks and pumped about fifty tons of water from the port to the starboard tanks.

In those days you had to make an entry in the engine room log showing the number of buckets of ashes thrown overboard during each watch underway, in order to indicate the quality of the coal you were burning. On my first midshipman's cruise I used to swing my hammock on the boat deck near the ash hoist from No. 1 fire room, and so I became acquainted with a regular ritual which occurred almost every night. Near midnight the steaming watch which was about to be relieved would clean fires, and would have a lot of ashes to hoist and throw overboard before the midwatch took over. I was awakened many a time about the middle of this operation by the coal heaver on deck, hollering down the ash hoist and inquiring, "How many buckets was that?" Invariably the voice from below replied, "I dunno, I thought you wuz counting them."

This was usually followed by the clatter of a large ash can dropping freely down the shaft all the way from the boat deck to the fire room, instead of descending more or less silently attached to the whip. After a resounding crash when the bucket hit the floor plates a voice on deck always yelled, "Look out below." What the voice from below replied cannot be recorded in this book.

Many changes have been made in engineering plants since those days. In the *Guadalcanal* we had high-pressure oil burning boilers and a strange kind of an engine, a Skinner five-cylinder, two-cycle reciprocating affair, using high-pressure steam in all cylinders and squirting lube oil into the steam as it enters the cylinders, a procedure which would have been unthinkable when I was a grease monkey in the *Maine*.

Steam is the life blood of a modern ship. Let's trace a little puff of steam on its travels through the ship engineering plant. It starts off as a drop of sea water which is suddenly jerked out of its peaceful nautical environment, sucked aboard the ship by one of the fire pumps and shoved into the evaporators. Here it's warmed up until it boils into steam, leaving its salt behind on the coils of the evaps, and going on its way to the distillers. In the distillers it is converted into fresh water by contact with tubes cooled by other little drops of sea water, whose sojourn in the ship is just long enough to be sucked in, sent through the distiller coils and then ejected overboard again.

From the distillers our now purified little drop of fresh water goes to the feed tanks of the ship to wait till it is needed in the boilers. When the time comes, a feed pump sends for it and pushes it through a heater where its temperature is again raised almost to the boiling point. Thence, still as water, it is forced through the feed lines to the boiler stop and check valve.

This is one of the critical points in the system, because the setting of this valve controls the amount of water admitted to the boiler, and if the valve is improperly regulated you can either blow up the boiler or wreck your engines. The water tender on watch in the fire room keeps a sharp eye on the boiler's gauge glass and regulates his check valve so that the water is neither too high nor too low. At the proper time the little drop of water slips through the check valve, into the boiler, and starts on the wildest binge of its young life.

As it circulates through the boiler its temperature is raised to nearly that of red hot metal, way above what it was in the evaporators. The white-hot oil fires on the outside of the boiler tubes, fanned by the whirring blowers which force air through the oil burners, and up the stack, keep adding heat to the little drop and raising its blood pressure until it finally bursts into superheated steam.

Now our drop goes berserk. It shoots through the boiler stop valve and down the main steam line, a pipe so hot it glows in the dark. It whirls through the bulkhead stop and into the engine room where the throttle valve regulates the amount of steam being admitted to the engine. The lad with his hand on this valve controls 8000 h.p. with a flip of his wrist. Any change in this valve setting changes the r.p.m. on the main shafts, and the speed of the ship.

After getting past the throttle valve our little drop plunges into the receiver which distributes steam to the five cylinders of the engine. Here it marks time impatiently, waiting for the intake valve to pop open at the proper point in the cycle so it can get into the cylinder and fulfill its destiny.

Up to this point all the heat energy stored in our drop by the boilers has been carefully conserved. The steam lines through which it has passed have been covered with asbestos to keep its heat in, and all flanges and joints have been set up tight to hold the high pressure.

In the cylinder our little puff of steam rams into the piston and suddenly finds its pressure falling. As it shoves against the inlet valve, which slammed shut behind it, and the piston, it finds that the piston gives. It drives the piston down, thus turning the main shaft and the propeller, and driving the ship one revolution closer to port.

During this downstroke one of the miracles of modern science is performed. In the boilers the chemical energy of the fuel oil was converted into heat energy and stored in the steam. In the engine the heat energy of the steam is converted into mechanical energy to move the ship.

When our little puff of steam emerges from the exhaust valve its temperature and blood pressure are again nearly normal. It is sucked into the condenser and cooled by its salty brothers circulating on the other side of the tubes, until it condenses into fresh water again in almost a complete vacuum, and complete state of exhaustion.

Having just gone through a Skinner uniflow engine it is now a rather greasy drop of water, totally unfit to be admitted into a self-respecting boiler where only the purest of water is allowed. So the main air pump, after sucking it out of the condenser, pushes it through a filter of Fuller's earth. I don't understand all I know about Fuller's earth, but I can assure you that so far as Earl Trosino and I are concerned, you can have the stuff. It was a constant pain in the neck to us, because if we took aboard enough of the damned stuff to purify the feed water, we would have had no room for airplanes. So our boilers sometimes just had to put up with a little grease.

Emerging from the filter our little drop goes back to the feed tank to catch its breath for a while after its recent exertions. It recuperates there until the feed pump picks it up and starts it on its mad way through the boiler to push the propeller around once more.

This goes on and on until our little drop either escapes through a leaky joint somewhere and drops into the bilges to be pumped overboard at the end of that watch, or perhaps escapes through a safety valve and goes off in a fluffy white cloud in the skies, until it eventually comes down as rain and rejoins its salty brothers in the ocean again.

Earl Trosino ruled over this realm we have just explored. Earl earned his ticket as chief engineer in the Merchant Marine, where you've got to be good to make the grade because the competition is tough, and a careless chief engineer can blow all the profits of a voyage up the stack in smoke. He knew how to stop trouble before it happened, and how to fix things at sea if trouble did sneak up on him.

Time and time again we had casualties to our plant which would have sent most ships limping into the nearest Navy yard. Earl used bailing wire, rubber bands, and sometimes, I think, black magic to make temporary repairs that always enabled us to complete our mission before heading for home.

He could step into a strange engine room, look at a tangled array of valves, pipes, and levers, and in the length of time it takes to tell about it, he knew how the whole business worked. His ability to do this enabled us to capture a foundering German submarine later on, and thus was instrumental in a historic day's work.

Earl had his troubles, as all chief engineers do. The minute the least puff of smoke came out of the stacks, the squawk box from the bridge would blare at him, "Stop Smoke." You don't want to advertise your position when you are stalking submarines.

In the course of a day's steaming, boiler tubes accumulate a lot of soot which the chief engineer wants to blow up the stack at night by speeding up his blowers; but if he does it when the wind is wrong, it were better had he not been born. The skipper, the Air Officer, and all the pilots will be after his hide the next morning when they find their airplanes on the flight deck looking like chimney sweeps. So, getting permission to blow tubes involves negotiating with the O.O.D. to find out if the wind is right, and further negotiations with the navigator and Captain to have it made right, if it isn't, by changing the course of the ship.

Polluting coastal waters with oil is almost a capital offense these days, so the chief had better get his bilges pumped and his empty fuel tanks flushed out before the navigator makes his landfall. While he is doing this pumping, thus shifting weight around, he is apt to put a list on the ship and to get a blast about this from the Air Officer and the Exec. He will probably blame the list on a strong wind abeam, or on the First Lieutenant, while he is hastily readjusting his ballast to bring the ship back on an even keel again.

Besides all these things, the chief has to worry about making fresh water for the washrooms and galley faster than a crew of drugstore cowboys can waste it. We tried to teach the boys to be frugal with fresh water, but we never rationed it except to the Nazi prisoners. *They* had to wash in salt water. After all, that's what they got in their own submarines, and besides, we were afraid that a sudden shift to fresh-water bathing might give them the itch or something. Dr. Monat, who was born and raised in France, and whose parents were imprisoned by the Nazis, gravely assured me that this was so.

When I was a midshipman on the *Maine* I had the value of fresh water impressed on me in a curious manner shortly after I got aboard. Fresh water was strictly rationed. You were allowed a half a bucket a day which was supposed to cover all your needs, including scrubbing your own clothes, and your name was checked off on the list when you drew your half-bucket.

On about my second day aboard, after standing in line

for an hour, I finally drew my precious allowance and lugged it down to the washroom to do my laundry.

In the washroom you could heat water by sticking your bucket under the open end of a small steam pipe, and with the end of the pipe submerged in the water, opening a valve and blowing live steam into your bucket until it was as hot as you wanted it.

But on this particular day, due to some monkey business with the valves in the engine room, this pipe, instead of having steam pressure inside it, had a strong vacuum in it. I hung my bucket in the proper place, opened the "steam" valve, and before I knew it, all my precious water had been sucked right out of the bucket and back into the ship's tanks!

I figured the chief engineer of that ship was an under-handed S.O.B.—but also a scientific one.

The engineers have a lingo all their own. For some obscure reason, the "log room," which you might expect to be the navigator's office, actually belongs to the chief engineer. If you spoke of an engine room "deck" or fire room "deck" you would give yourself away as a complete greenhorn. "Floor plates" is the word. A boiler is a "can." You "light it off" and "cut it in" on the "main line" when the steaming watch has been set prior to getting underway.

An experienced engine room hand describes a worn bearing by saying, "It has enough clearence for a big rat to crawl through it," and mentally makes a note to take some of the shims out of the bearing cap as soon as the plant is shut down. His method of expressing utter contempt for a very ignorant person is to say, "He don't know whether his ear holes are punched or bored."

A real engineer always carries a monkey wrench in his pocket to set up on leaky flanges, glands or gaskets, and also, of course, because standard Navy remedy No. 1 for fixing any piece of faulty machinery is, "First try tapping it with a monkey wrench." Many a pump has resumed normal operation after a light smack on the cylinder head or valve stem with this useful instrument.

Another necessary piece of equipment for an engineer to carry is a rag; although he will settle for a handful of waste if he can't get a nice clean rag. Otherwise the only way he can wipe the grease off his hands is on the seat of his pants. It takes bales and bales of rags to keep a ship running right, and woe betide the paymaster who runs out of rags in the middle of a cruise.

The engineers are not glamour boys, like the gunners and aviators. You seldom see their pictures in the papers, and they don't get the citations and medals that the topside boys do. But very often, were it not for the engineers, those citations and medals would be posthumous. When the kamikaze menace was at its height, several of our big carriers were turned into roaring furnaces from the hangar deck up by Japs diving their planes into our ships. In several cases it looked like the ships were doomed, and that the only sensible thing to do was to have all hands who could still do so abandon ship before it was too late. These ships were saved because the engineers stuck to their posts and kept the machinery running, enabling their shipmates topside to eventually control the fire and save the ship.

The boys on deck did heroic work, of course. But it's one thing to be a hero if you know that when the ship capsizes just before making her final plunge you will have a battling chance of getting overboard and swimming away from it. It takes a different kind of guts to stick to your post down in the bowels of the ship when choking fumes pour down the "ventilators"; when you can hear and feel the heavy explosions tearing the ship apart above you; when you've got to hang on to keep from sliding down the slanting floor plates as the ship takes a list and her period of roll gets ominously longer. Down there you haven't got a chance if she rolls over. Nine times out of ten, even if the word is passed to abandon ship, you probably won't get it. That word is never passed until the ship is *in extremis,* by which time all communications are usually gone.

I could spend hours showing you around down below, but we had better get back up on deck. As we emerge from the engine room hatch, let me quote Kipling again: "Lord, send a man like Robbie Burns to sing the Song o' Steam!"

As we emerge from the engine room we are still far down below in the ship; just below the water line, in fact. It is here that most of the community life of the ship goes on. The messing and sleeping compartments are located on this level, as well as the galley, butcher shop, washrooms, and most of the incidental shops which any modern community needs.

On most ships nowadays each man has a bunk and locker instead of the sailor's traditional bag and hammock. The bunks are standee affairs four deep. A sailor's bunk and locker are the only things on a ship which he can call his own, except on submarines, where, as one man hits the deck to go on watch, another man coming off watch crawls into the same sack. This is known as the "hot bunk system."

Our present-day ships have a laundry, cobbler shop, barbershop, tailor shop and soda fountain. For some reason, understood only by U.S. Navy enlisted men, the products of the soda fountain are known as "Geedunks."

Last, by not least, every large ship has a "Ship's Service Store." This emporium is stocked with all kinds of stuff such as earrings, watches, necklaces, brooches and silk stockings. This merchandise may seem rather incongruous in a ship's store, but the sailors call it "poogie bait" and claim it is very useful.

Modern science has wrought many changes topside as well as down below. Radio has stripped the skipper of some of the initiative and responsibility which was his in the old days. In a sailing ship the Captain became an independent sovereign as soon as the shore line dropped out of sight astern. He had to work out his own answers to unexpected situations as best he could. Now, radio ties him to the apron strings of the Navy Department no matter where he is. Even under conditions of radio silence, you still have to keep a listening watch for incoming orders even though you might be excused from replying to them.

The communicators are a group who sometimes hold the fate of the ship in their hands. They have to listen around the clock to all the coded gibberish which fills the air, and sort out the messages carrying the call sign of their ship. They sit in the radio shack apparently half-asleep, automatically copying all the stuff they hear. They eventually get so that the dots and dashes come in through their ears, bypass their brains, and come out of their pencils as letters by reflex action. But their own ship's call in the jumble of dots and dashes flowing through their consciousness is like a fire alarm bell. It snaps them out of their lethargy, because during radio silence they can't ask for a repeat, and if they miss a single dot or dash it will cause a garble when the message is decoded; a garble which might result in disaster.

You are only supposed to decode those messages which are specifically addressed to you, even though you are required to copy everything you hear. However, there are ways by which you can recognize particularly important messages which have red-hot dope in them. Human nature being what it is, communication watch officers usually violate the rules and decode *all* top secret messages just to see what is in them. They say, "Maybe it's something we ought to know." You might just as well try to stop your neighbors from listening in on a party line.

I put the blast on my communicators a number of times for violating the rules and bringing me hot stuff which they shouldn't have decoded. I always read these messages and learned a lot of interesting things that way, because how could I tell that I shouldn't have read the message unless I *did* read it and find out what was in it? After being bawled out for this, the watch officers finally quit bringing these messages to me although I am practically sure they kept on breaking all top secrets. But even so, I accomplished some good by my tirades, because the watch officers who decoded unauthorized messages felt so guilty about it that they didn't dare share their tidbits of news with anyone else in the ship. And if they had told me I probably couldn't have resisted the temptation to tell Jesse Johnson and Bikkers—in strict confidence of course—and each of them would have done likewise, etc., down the line until even the Captain of the Head knew all about it.

There are three sounds of World War II which will stand out in my memory among all the noises of the world, as long as I live. One is the eerie wail of the air raid warning sirens in London during the blitz, when I was an observer there before we got in the war. If the Nazis had specified the pitch, cadence, tempo and volume of those sirens in order to strike terror into the hearts of their hearers they couldn't have made a shrewder choice. The second unforgettable tune is a yodeling sound on certain radio frequencies which I heard every day up in Iceland and all over the Atlantic Ocean in the *Guadalcanal*. We called it "the bagpipes," and figured it was an attempt by the Krauts to jam our communications. The third one is the unearthly, high-pitched whine of a motor generator for our radio transmitters, which was mounted on the other side of the bulkhead from my bunk in the sea cabin of the *Guadalcanal*. Every night at sea, when I tried to relax and get some much needed sleep, that goddam motor generator sang me a nerve-racking "lullaby" that would have awakened Rip Van Winkle. But eventually I got so used to it that one night when it burned out a bearing and stopped I woke up immediately.

There is an old story among seafaring men about a lighthouse keeper, who spent his life tending the light on an isolated rock. Every night before going to bed he set the clockwork mechanism which fired a signal gun at midnight, so passing ships could correct their chronometers. For forty years the gun fired without fail at the exact instant that the local mean sun crossed the lower limb of the meridian. Finally one night the gun failed to fire.

The old lighthouse keeper snapped out of a sound sleep, sat bolt upright in his bunk and said, "What was that?"

I know exactly how he felt.

On the way up to the flight deck we pass the brain of the ship, the Combat Information Center. The C.I.C. is full of radar scopes, high-frequency radio transmitters, squawk boxes, dead-reckoning tracers, status boards, and verticle display plots. It is like a broadcasting studio, stock broker's office, bookmaking establishment, and airport control tower all rolled into one. All information flows in through C.I.C.; is evaluated and displayed there; and the orders to meet changes in the current situation are flashed out from this point. The Fighter Director Officer is the announcer and master of ceremonies for this show. He needs a level head, nimble wit and sometimes a sharp tongue to ride herd over the air group and keep them on the beam.

The Fighter Directors also have a jargon all their own. If they tell you to "orbit tomcat under mattress angels six," they mean to circle the picket destroyer under the clouds of six thousand feet. "Bandit closing, vector zero niner zero, buster" tells you that they have an enemy aircraft approaching on their scope and that you must fly east at full gun in order to "tallyho." If, while enroute to intercept this plane, you should be jumped on by enemy fighters, you grab your mike and raise the traditional rallying cry of the carnivals, "Hey Rube!"

When an air group returns from an eventful combat mission they are apt to be so full of what they have done that as soon as they sight the ship they want to tell the world about it. Unless your controller in C.I.C. enforces radio discipline with an iron hand the radio channels will soon sound like feeding time in the birdhouse at the zoo.

The flyers aren't the only ones who sometimes get too gabby on the radio. Every task group has a T.B.S. circuit (Talk Between Ships), reserved for tactical signals from the Admiral to his Captains. The Admiral will occasionally test this circuit by sending out a general call and asking

"How do you hear me?" Each ship replies by giving two numbers taken from a code table which indicate the volume and clarity of their reception on the Admiral's test message. "Five by Five" is the reply which indicates that everything is hunky-dory.

In the middle of the war a new ship reported to Admiral Jerry Bogan's task group operating off Tokyo. To be sure he didn't miss anything that was going on the skipper sent Admiral Bogan a test message each morning at sunrise asking, "How do you hear me—over."

About the third morning the reply came back from the flagship: "I hear you two by two. Too often and too long."

In the past, whenever anything unusual happened at sea, the Captain hurried up to the bridge to have a look-see. Now, many Captains head for C.I.C., instead of the bridge, because you can actually "see" more there. The large vertical plotting board in C.I.C, shows the present position of all planes in the air, whether they are friendly, hostile, or unidentified; of other ships; of land; and a great deal of other information. It is continuously corrected up to the minute as the radar antenna sweeps around the horizon.

You can glance at a radar scope and "see" another ship twenty miles away on a dark and foggy night. If you were straining your eyes through the fog on the bridge, you might not *see* this ship until just before you collided with it. By radar you can "see" an approaching enemy bomber a hundred miles away while there is still time to organize a reception committee if you work fast. But if you wait till you see him with your eyes, it's too late to do anything but lead out the fire hoses and alert the stretcher bearers. However, custom dies hard, and some of the current generation of skippers still stick to the bridge. As radar and television improve, what you see with your eyes becomes less and less important. The Captains of the atomic age will place the deck in C.I.C. instead of the bridge when the heat is on.

Dick Kane, our Air Officer, presided over the C.I.C. and

also over the hangar deck and flight deck. I liked the cut of Dick's jib right down from the beginning. He was a "Can Do" guy, who was much better at finding ways of doing tough jobs than at finding reasons why they couldn't be done.

He was responsible, among many other things, for the training of the flight deck crew. This puts the Air Officer on the spot, because the skipper, being an aviator himself, thinks he knows more about running a flight deck than any young punk air officer.

When planes are taking off or landing, the skipper has nothing else to do but stand on the bridge and kibitz. He views operations from the same point of vantage as a spotter in the press box at a football game. The big difference is that when the spotter phones his observations down to the coach on the bench, his stuff is merely advisory. But the skipper's comments on flight deck operations usually are peremptory orders originating about one foot from the Air Officer's ear.

But Dick Kane knew all the tricks of the trade, and was usually half a jump ahead of me whenever I thought I had caught him off base.

Landing an air group on a carrier is a beautiful sight to see when the flight deck crew knows their stuff. An incoming plane is snubbed up short by the arresting gear; the barriers drop; the hook man dives under the tail and disengages the arresting wire; the taxi director dances up the deck backwards waving his hands over his head; the pilot gives her a burst of gun and the plane boils out of the landing area. The wires snap back to the arresting position; barriers go up; and "Fly two" flashes the all-clear signal back to the Landing Signal Officer, just in time to give the "cut" signal, and bring the next plane in with a fifteen-second interval.

By fast work in dropping a barrier, an operator who is on his toes can often save ruining a propeller when a plane floats up the deck and hooks the last wire. On the other hand, a barrier operator who jumps the gun can cause a

146

bad crash by dropping his barrier before a plane has actually hooked a wire. Apparently Dick worked those barriers by mental telepathy.

Snappy work by a good taxi director and enthusiastic use of the throttle by a pilot who has just landed can prevent many a wave-off by quickly clearing the landing area for the next plane coming up the groove.

Some day a great ballet will be written around operations on a carrier flight deck. A well-drilled flight deck crew in action is poetry in motion. All orders to the planes on deck are given in pantomime. These signals will go right into the ballet unchanged. The planes will be ballerinas, asleep on deck when the curtain rises. Plane captains will awaken them, and as they "warm up" the music will rise to a crescendo. As "Fly one" waves the highball each plane in turn will take off into the wings, and as the music resumes its normal pitch, the flight deck crews dance around getting the deck ready for landing. As the planes later fly in from backstage and land, the deck crews will expertly disengage them from the arresting gear and the plane handlers will lead them quickly to their parking spots and cut their engines. As his plane gets back, each plane captain will prance out from the wings and solicitously check her over.

The landing signal officer with his flags will do a dance that will bring down the house. I've often seen him do it trying to bring down a plane when the ship had a lot of motion on her.

The music for this fantasy must have salty air about it, must have twenty-five knots of wind blowing through it, and the bass will be the full-throated roar of powerful engines.

I want to be on hand in a box seat for the première of this ballet when it is produced. Until it is produced, I'll settle for a place on the bridge looking down on the flight deck of an *Essex* class carrier when the air group and plane handlers are in the groove. The Ballet Russe can't sail within several points of that performance.

We had trouble teaching the boys not to wander out on the flight deck when operations were going on. When a sailor wants to get from one side of the ship to the other he usually takes the straightforward method of simply strolling across the deck. This is O.K. on most ships, but not on a carrier. If you want to get from one side of a flight deck to the other, you should use a passageway that goes *under* the deck, even though this may involve a few additional steps.

We preached about this for weeks without getting any appreciable results. Jaywalkers ofter wandered out on the flight deck just as a heavily-loaded plane was about to land. We finally solved this problem in half a day at the cost of one bushel of potatoes.

During flight operations there were always a lot of spectators up in the island. We put a basket of potatoes at a convenient spot and declared open season on jaywalkers.

The first trespasser to meander out on the flight deck that morning was straddled by a salvo of spuds, several of which caught him smack in the aft. As he whirled around indignantly to confront his assailant, a high velocity potato bopped him right on the beak.

In no time at all word got around all over the ship that it wasn't "safe" any more to venture out on the flight deck while operations were in progress.

The main battery of this great warship of ours consisted of one five-inch gun. This was mounted on the stern, and would not bear forward of the beam—a pretty clear indication that if we met the *Tirpitz* we were expected to entice her into a running battle rather than slug it out with yardarm to yardarm.

At the Battle of San Bernadino Strait the Jap battleships caught our jeep carrier task group flatfooted, and opened up on them with their sixteen-inch guns. As the battlewagons closed in for the kill, and huge geysers of water, caused by shells from their main batteries were spouting up all around the *Gambier Bay,* the gun captain of her lone five-inch gun is reliably reported to have said, "Don't worry, fellows, we're sucking them in to 40 mm. range!"

A few minutes later the Guardian Angel of jeep carriers somehow pulled the wool over the Jap Admiral's eyes and convinced him that these were *Essex* class carriers he was tangling with. So he reversed course and ran for Japan! As our dumfounded skippers gaped at the Jap battleships scurrying off over the horizon and breathed prayers of thanks for their miraculous deliverance, some young joker on the flight deck of the *Fanshaw Bay* yelled up to the bridge, "Better watch 'em, Cap'n—or they'll get away!"

The Jeeps had an antiaircraft battery of 40 mm, pom-poms and 20 mm. guns. Balloon busting was quite a sport for these guns. We released aerological balloons from the flight deck, and the gun crews competed to see which could burst the balloons with the least number of shots. Our champion crew was No. 6 20 mm. gun, manned entirely by colored mess boys, and they took fierce pride in defending their laurels at each shot. When I called the winning crew up to the bridge to congratulate them at the end of the shoot, you could read things in the shining eyes of those colored boys that would fill a book.

I had specialized in ordnance for many years, and occasionally when the experts disagreed I was called upon as the final responsible authority to settle the argument. I am stuck with one of these decisions for the rest of my life.

There was some question about how the safety wires should be rigged on our aircraft depth charges. I refereed the final argument about this and decided in favor of the way our ship's gunner wanted to rig them. As the conference broke up, the gunner said to me, "Cap'n, I'll bet my life on that rig." I felt the same way about it.

Next day the gunner went out in one of our torpedo planes to make a test drop. Just after take-off the engine quit, but the plane made a successful water landing only a few hundred yards from the ship. As we headed over to pick up the boys we saw all three climb out of the cockpit and stand on the wings. Before we got there the depth charges exploded.

There were no survivors. We recovered one body, which we buried at sea that same afternoon. I stood with my head bowed at the funeral services and wished that I hadn't been called in on that argument.

CHAPTER 8

"SPURLOS VERSUNKT"

The *Guadalcanal* shoved off on her first war cruise from Norfolk on January 2, 1944. With our four escort destroyers and our airgroup, VC-13, we formed Task Group 22.3, operating directly under Admiral Ingersoll, Commander in Chief, Atlantic Fleet.

Admiral Ingersoll was a grand man to work for, because he believed in giving you a little leeway in your orders. Many Admirals, instead of just telling you what they want you to do, will go into a lot of details about how your are to do it too. Admiral Ingersoll's dispatch to me said, "Operate against enemy submarines in the North Atlantic." That gave me a job to do, and an area to work in, but left me a few of the details to work out on my own hook. Those sorts of orders put the whole business right in your lap. The Admiral was in effect saying, "I've given you adequate forces to do the job; I am authorizing you to proceed into submarine waters; I have confidence in your judgment—get going." If you come back empty-handed when you have been operating under those orders you can't blame your boss.

For the year previous to this the *Card* and the *Bogue,* the first two CVE's to appear in the Atlantic, had been hanging up fabulous records, and blazing a trail for the rest of us to follow. Early in the war the Atlantic Ocean outside the range of shore-based aircraft had been practically a submarine sanctuary. The range of shore-based aircraft had been constantly increasing, but in 1943 there was still a large area in the middle of the Atlantic which these aircraft couldn't reach, and where the subs used to bask on the surface taking sun baths all day long. They knew that no aircraft could surprise them in that area and, so far as surface craft were concerned, the subs always sighted them first and did the surprising.

Early in 1943 the *Card* and the *Bogue* invaded this area like a couple of hungry wolves turned loose in a pasture among a flock of tame sheep. One afternoon the *Card's* airplanes barged into a group of five U-boats on the surface holding a sort of a convention and sunning themselves. It took them a long time to realize that the honeymoon was over, and that even one thousand miles from the nearest land, small, fast airplanes might swoop down out of the clouds and blast them to the bottom. About twenty subs went to the bottom in the "sanctuary" area before the Nazis knew what was hitting them. In some way these little airplanes were more deadly to the subs than the larger shore-based aircraft, because they were flown by pilots who were seamen as well as airmen, and were better trained as submarine hunters. They were at home over salt water, and didn't mind getting down close enough to it to make sure of what they saw, and to do an effective job on a sturdy hulled sub.

Until the word got around in the Nazi U-boat fleet that our CVE's had closed the gap in the middle of the ocean, the *Card* and the *Bogue* had happy hunting. The *Card,* commanded by my classmate, Buster Isbell, got over ten kills in her first year and earned the coveted Presidential Unit Citation. The first thing I did when the *Guadalcanal* got to Norfolk was to go aboard the *Card,* sit at Buster's feet, ask a few questions and listen for a whole afternoon. Buster confirmed a lot of things which I had figured out for myself, but I was a long way from being sure of them until I got the word from the master craftsman in person.

Buster came through some hairy situations during his year in the Atlantic, and eluded all the perils of the deep which came at him from below. A year later, when he was an innocent bystander on the "makey learn" cruise in the *Franklin,* prior to taking over command on one of our big carriers in the Pacific, he died in the blazing furnace which Japanese bombs kindled on the Big Ben. The Nazis couldn't touch him from below—but the Japs got him from above.

In addition to talking to Buster and getting the real low-down, I read all the reports of other CVE's which were operating in the Atlantic at that time. Some of them scared me much worse than German subs ever did. By this time the Germans had become very cautious and the hunting was scarce, but you would never guess it from reading the reports which some of the boys wrote. There was one ship in particular which, according to her reports, was surrounded by the Nazi U-boat Navy every night and—like the late W. C. Fields, had to "fight her way out through a wall of living flesh . . . dragging her canoe behind her." She emerged victorious at dawn each day, claiming every disappearing radar blip and every sonar contact on a school of fish, as a certain kill. After reading these reports I approached our first foray into the snake pit with fear and trembling.

The Nazi submarines which we were fighting at this time were the old-type U-boats, not to be confused with the present day snorkel submarine, a totally different and more elusive breed of sharks. The old-type submarines spent most of their time on the surface and submerged only when forced to do so by approaching planes or destroyers; or when they were making their own attacks on convoys. While on the surface they ran on Diesel engines, for which they carried a three-months' supply of fuel. When submerged they couldn't run their Diesels because, in the pre-snorkel days, there was no way to supply air to them, so the U-boats had to run on storage batteries and electric motors.

Even the huge submarine storage batteries were good for only about twenty-four hours of continuous operation; at the end of that time they had to be recharged. The sub had to come up to the surface and run on her Diesels to do this. Since the U-boat skippers never knew when they might be attacked they all liked to cruise around with fully charged batteries so they could submerge for twenty-four hours if necessary to shake off pursuers. The only way they could keep their batteries fully charged and ready for emergencies was to run surfaced for normal cruising. In addition, the sub's purpose in life was to find and sink merchant ships, and finding them was often a tougher job than sinking them. You can find them very much better with half a dozen lookouts aloft in the conning tower fifteen feet above the water, than you can with a periscope just clearing the troughs of the waves. As a result, the old type U-boats spent perhaps ninety-five per cent of its time on the surface. This was the key to our anti-submarine tactics at that time.

The most effective way of finding the old-type submarines was by eye from the air, after you had learned how to look for them and how to distinguish them from the many other things that inhabit the sea. Radar was useful too, and so was the pinging and listening gear of our destroyers; but we still relied principally on our planes because they could search wide areas quickly.

Stalking submarines is big-game hunting for ferocious, man-and-ship-eating beasts, but most of the time it is monotonous and discouraging drudgery. Your planes scour the ocean continuously, with the ship's gun crews practically living at their stations. You must constantly ready to shoot fast and accurately or you may turn out to be game instead of hunter.

For weeks at a time nothing may happen except perhaps a false alarm, when the lads get desperate from boredom and begin imagining things. But if you look for trouble long enough you will usually find it, and when you do pick up a hot trail and know it's the McCoy, the news goes through the ship like an electric shock. All hands know that from then on the chips are down and they're playing for keeps.

The sub is a wily quarry. Her lookouts know their lives depend on alertness, too, and so, more often than not, they spot your planes in time to give warning for a crash dive before they can be knocked out from the air. However, in 1944, a sub's underwater speed was very slow. If the planes were able to report an actual sighting, your search could focus on a small area where the destroyers' listening gear was effective. But even though the sub's submerged speed was low the U-boat did move, and the area of search grew in size until darkness came along. Then the sub might decide to surface and run for it at high speed using his Diesels. During the early years of the Battle of the Atlantic, he could usually get away with this at night. But after we equipped our planes with radar and learned how to operate from carriers at night, we could spot subs on the surface even in the dark.

A hot chase might last for days, with planes getting several fleeting glimpses of the crash-diving sub, with sound contacts picked up, held awhile, and lost again by the destroyers, with numerous depth charge attacks which may or may not do serious damage. Then suddenly the sea opens up and a huge black shape heaves itself to the surface, white water pouring off its sides. Your quarry is at bay. Sometimes she comes up fighting, striking out wildly in all directions during her final agony. Other times the hatches pop open and small black figures go plunging over the side.

When a cornered sub does surface, all hell bursts loose. You can't stand on ceremony and wait for him to initiate negotiations leading to a possible surrender. Your destroyers charge in at full speed zigzagging wildly and blazing away with everything they've got. Your planes swoop down with the machine guns snarling like hounds worrying a bear. Depth charges, rockets, armor-piercing projectiles, and torpedoes rip into the surfaced sub from all directions. Maybe that U-boat came up to surrender, but you can't afford to jump to any conclusions; the penalty for being wrong is too severe. You've got to let him have it.

A wounded sub within five miles of you is an extremely

dangerous animal. Her torpedoes can turn a fine ship into a blazing shambles. A salvo of six fish, fired just as the crew abandons the sub, will scurry about with their doses of sudden death for approximately twenty minutes. You never know whether your cornered enemy is going to fight or not. But you do know that he has a knockout punch left, and you don't want to be in the way if he swings it.

Submarine hunting is a difficult trade for aviators, too, and requires highly specialized training. At the Battle of Midway one of our Air Force bomber pilots reported plastering a "large Japanese cruiser" from high altitude and seeing it "sink without a trace in half a minute." When our submarine *Grayling* returned to Honolulu a few days later her crew made profane and salty remarks about lubberly aviators who couldn't tell a Jap heavy cruiser from a U.S. submarine.

This brings out an important fact of anti-submarine warfare. Naturally every submarine in healthy condition "sinks" the moment he is attacked by aircraft, because a crash dive makes him invisible and at least temporarily immune from further attack. Aviators are notoriously over-optimistic in scoring the accuracy of their own bombing attacks, so when an aviator finally attacks a submarine after weeks of scouring an empty ocean, and actually sees his submarine "sink," you can bet both your anchors he is going to emphatically and honestly claim a kill.

For this reason the Navy Department established the Anti-Submarine Warfare Assessment Board in Washington to evaluate all anti-submarine attacks and score them officially as "sunk," "probably sunk," "probably damaged," etc. The most disillusioned bunch of skeptics in the world sat on this board. Not one of them would believe his own mother under oath unless she could produce photographs, oil samples, or prisoners.

When I was up in Iceland early in the war I personally pulled the bomb release on two attacks which I *know* sank submarines, but to this day the Navy Department won't admit this. (Of course, my case is the exception that proves the rule about aviators being over-optimistic about their own efforts!)

One of the tools of the trade employed by sub-hunting aviators is the sonobuoy, a device for eavesdropping on the ocean. You toss it overboard from a plane and this busy little gadget floats, lowers a microphone several fathoms into the deep, sticks up a radio antenna, listens down below and broadcasts what it hears.

However, the sonobuoy, like a parrot, simply repeats what it hears. *You* have to decide what it means. Sometimes you hear the screws of your own ship. Certain kinds of fish make rhythmic croaking noises, and breaking waves are noisy. An eager and imaginative young aviator can hear anything he wants to hear badly enough, especially if he has been flying around over the ocean for several weeks without seeing or hearing anything.

One day one of my lads reported hearing the screws of the task group at a distance of fifty miles. I didn't believe it, but he insisted, so I told him on the radio: "We will stop all ships for five minutes. . . . Listen, and tell us what happens."

For the next fifteen minutes he heard every move that we claimed we made. When I told him we had started again, he noted it right away. Whenever I told him we had started or stopped, he was Johnny on the spot and heard it. The only hitch was that we had never made any change whatsoever in the course or speed of the task group.

I am sure that if I had told the boys that every submarine carried a brass band which played "Deutschland uber alles" all day long, one of them would have finally heard this over a sonobuoy.

Sonar is the underwater equivalent of radar. You make a *ping* in the water and listen for a return echo indicating that there is something out there besides the empty ocean. But you can't always tell what that something is. When you do get an echo it may be a layer of cold water, it may be a knuckle in your own wake. A dense school of fish or a whale can fool inexperienced operators. I've even heard tell of one task group in which the sonar operators were completely befuddled by noises which were later traced to a pair of breeding whales.

Radar contacts can fool you badly too. You sometimes have "ghosts" on radar scopes. I have listened to some very scientific explanations of these phenomena by experts, but as far as I'm concerned, they are simply the electronic version of gremlins. One of the most difficult decisions an anti-submarine task group commander has to make it what to do about a tiny blip that dances around on the scope for a while and then disappears. If it is a diving sub the task group should drop everything else it is doing and stay with that contact till they get him. But if you jump to a hasty conclusion, you may spend the next two weeks chasing a will-o'-the-wisp.

On numerous occasions out in the Atlantic a tense group of officers have huddled around a radar scope anxiously watching the skipper's face as the Old Man made up his mind. They thought he was carefully evaluating all their expert advice and methodically arriving at the most logical conclusion. What he was actually doing, as often as not, was mentally flipping a nickel.

In addition to those gremlins which got into your radar scopes more or less spontaneously, the subs had a way of producing ghosts artificially. They would surface at night and release small balloons attached to a cork float which remained on the surface. These balloons had strips of tin foil attached to them and produced almost exactly the same kind of intermittent radar echo as a submarine periscope. They made a perfect disappearing blip, and on a dark night they often convinced you that you had caught a sub in the act of taking a last look at you through his periscope just before firing his torpedoes.

Of course the tip-off on this phony was that it always drifted downwind, at a little bit less than the speed of the wind. But many a skipper spent a nerve-racking night zigzagging around one of these elusive wraiths, only to find a silly Nazi balloon leering at him when the sun came up.

All this simply proves that you can't believe everything that you think you hear or see when chasing submarines. If you add up all the attacks during the war on which aviators and destroyer skippers swear that they sank submarines beyond possibility of doubt, the total would equal the entire Nazi U-boat fleet multiplied by about ten. Those sons-of-bitches on the Assessment Board may have been a necessary evil after all. At the end of the war we found their scoring had been remarkably accurate.

Enroute to the Azores on our first cruise we passed Bermuda and decided to stop in there, to top off with fuel.

This visit to Bermuda resulted in my getting my tail feathers slightly scorched. We arrived off the entrance buoy just at sunset, and I was planning to get in that evening, refuel that night, and be on our way to the wars at the crack of dawn.

I failed to allow for the fact that Bermuda is a leisurely, easygoing place a long way from the battle front. They only fought the war from sunrise to sunset there.

As I was about to turn into the channel I received a blinker message saying, "Remain outside until 0800 tomorrow morning."

We spent that night zigzagging around within sight of the beach under a full moon and burning up oil, which was in short supply at home. My temperature rose with every zig and finally about midnight my safety valve lifted.

I sent a radio to Commander in Chief, Atlantic Fleet, telling how we were spending the night and why, and indicating that I took a dim view of it. I rashly made Commander Naval Operating Base, Bermuda, an information addressee on this dispatch and then turned in till sunrise.

When we anchored in Bermuda the next morning the Admiral's aide scrambled up the gangway before the splash from our anchor had subsided and informed me that I was to report to the Commandant *immediately*. It was a very angry Admiral who waved that dispatch under my nose in Headquarters and demanded an explanation of this breach of naval etiquette. It didn't pacify him a bit when I naïvely informed him that I had assumed from the leisurely tempo of things that the British were still running the place and that I thought I was putting *them* on the report.

After giving me a thorough sandblasting the Admiral filled our ships up with oil and bundled us out of there as fast as he could, and we didn't stick our nose into Bermuda again for six months. When we did, as will appear later in this yarn, all was forgiven and we were welcomed like prodigal sons.

Since we were the first Kaiser CVE to appear in the Atlantic, and everybody was still pretty skeptical about us, a lot depended on this first cruise of ours. If we got off to a bad start by cracking up a lot of airplanes or coming home empty-handed, it might damn the whole class of ships. We got two strikes on us right off the bat by killing one of the most experienced pilots in our new squadron in a crash that never should have happened. It was a little bit his fault, a little bit our fault, and ninety per cent bad luck. But the worst thing that can happen to a ship is to get a reputation for being unlucky.

So I was pretty jittery for a while after that. You can always look back after any accident and say, "If I had only done so-and-so, it wouldn't have happened," and you don't sleep well for a while after you see a couple of your lads disappear in a big splash right in front of your face, for no good reason.

But we were very lucky, indeed, that first cruise from then on. Other CVE's had made three or four cruises before getting their first U-boat kill. We hit the jackpot within two weeks.

Our aerial patrol caught a large "milch cow" submarine refueling a smaller one on the surface one evening just before sunset about forty miles from the task group. We got 'em completely by surprise and plastered the mother and pup with rockets and depth charges. The little domestic scene suddenly became a shambles of wreckage, oil, and struggling survivors.

It was like shooting fish in a barrel. The fully surfaced subs, encumbered by fuel hoses and towlines, could do nothing to counter or evade our attack. They met the same kind of fate that they usually dealt out to helpless merchant ships.

We immediately detached a destroyer to pick up survivors, but by the time she reached the area, it was a black and blustery night. It would have been almost impossible to find the men in the water even under favorable conditions after a long run to a vaguely fixed position. In this case the destroyer didn't dare show lights because our flyers reported that a third sub at the refueling party had gotten away. Our destroyer searched the area for several hours in the darkness but found nothing. Sometime during the night watches the "survivors" rejoined their U-boats down in Davy Jones's locker.

There are widows and orphans in Germany now as a result of that attack, but you never think of that until the war is over. If we had fumbled our chances there would be more widows and orphans in the U.S. than we have now.

We regretted our failure to rescue these men for two reasons: first, it's the law of the sea to rescue your enemy, if you can, after you've sunk his ship; and second, those skeptics in Washington.

On the basis of convincing photographs the Assessment Board eventually gave us grudging credit for sinking one sub and damaging the other. However, we couldn't wait that long, so we proudly painted two little Nazi flags on the side of our bridge that very evening.

Right after the attack came the most hectic hour and a half I've ever spent aboard ship. We had eight planes in the air and were just getting ready to swing into the wind and start landing them when one pair of planes barged

161

into the refueling party about forty miles from the task group and put the blast on it. This happened just a few minutes before sunset.

At this time we had not yet learned to land in the dark. So the important thing after the attack was to get our planes aboard before darkness descended on us. However, everybody in the air wanted to hop over and take a gander at the twenty or thirty Nazis swimming around among the wreckage. No amount of yelling at them on the radio could stop them. The rubberneck instinct is hard to curb. When we finally started landing planes it was getting pretty dark. The fifth plane to land couldn't see the deck very well, landed too far to starboard and fetched up with both wheels down in the gallery walkway which goes around the flight deck about four feet below the level of the flight deck. His tail stuck out athwartships across the deck, fouling the arresting gear.

We had to get him out of there—and fast. But we couldn't budge that damned plane. We couldn't drag it back on deck and we couldn't shove it overboard, and in the meantime the sun had gone down, leaving us under a solid overcast where it was darker than the inside of a hold. No amount of heaving, hauling, cursing, grunting, or praying would move that plane. We even tried listing the ship by whipping her into a tight turn under full rudder, but it was no good. We fell way short of our "Can Do" motto that night while it got blacker and blacker and our three circling planes drank up their low gas supply.

As time began running out on us and it became obvious that we weren't going to get that plane out of there we decided in desperation that maybe we could just ignore it. We told the three planes in the air that if they favored the port side a little bit when they landed their wing tips would clear the projecting tail and everything would be O.K.

But the pilots weren't quite as confident about this as we claimed that we were. For the next fifteen minutes they made the wildest swipes at a flight deck I've ever seen. After a dozen frantic wave-offs one of them finally wandered over somewhere near the center line of the deck and we "cut" him, even though he was much too fast. He hit the deck skidding to port, bounced into the air, rolled over on his back, and plunged into the sea. Our plane guard destroyer rescued all three aircrewmen, but that settled any idea of landing the other planes aboard.

There was nothing left to do but land them in the water. You've got to have lights to make a safe landing in the water at night but you don't want to show lights when a submarine is reported to be lurking just over the horizon. This was one of the times when we had to rely on our morning prayer. There's no use doing things halfway so we lighted the task group up like a waterfront saloon on Saturday night and ordered the pilots to ditch the planes. All of our people were fished out of the water safe and sound. We doused our lights and zigzagged to beat hell.

That hour after sunset was a preview in miniature of the wildest rat race in the history of naval aviation which was to occur a couple of months later on the other side of the world. After the Marianas Turkey Shoot where Admiral Pete Mitscher's fast carrier task group shot down over four hundred Jap planes, his air groups were caught out at sunset about two hundred miles from their parent carriers. There were 216 of our planes milling around in the dark for the next couple of hours. Half of them wound up in the water.

As the destroyers fished my boys out of the Atlantic that night, I promised myself two things: First, our flight deck crews were going to learn how to clear a crash from the deck; and second, we were going to learn how to get aboard in the dark.

Later that night we had a hair-raising battle with what I think now was a whale. The international recognition signal for whales, surfacing and blowing, is not visible at night. In a destroyer's underwater sound detector a whale gives almost the same kind of an echo as a submarine, especially if you have just gone through the ordeal that we had right after sunset. About midnight the destroyers sounded the alarm and scattered ash cans all over the ocean. Red flashes from their Y guns stabbed through the inky darkness and the sea rumbled and shook beneath us.

You feel conspicuous and naked at a time like this. You see nothing but blackness but you are certain in your own mind that the submarine is looking right smack down your throat with his periscope. It's the same idea as walking through a graveyard on a dark night. You have a feeling that things which you can't see are watching you.

It's even worse if you are down in the engine room and can feel the floor plates tremble when the depth charges go off. A torpedo hit up forward would make them tremble the same way. Earl Trosino claims that the *Guadalcanal's* engines *never* made more than 200 r.p.m. wide open. But a cagey engineer like Earl always keeps at least ten revolutions up his sleeve, hoping the skipper doesn't know about them. I don't care what Earl, or even the builders of the engines may say now; I found out by watching the indicators on the bridge that night that those engines will make 215 r.p.m. if the chief engineer is really scared.

A couple of days later we had a spectacular fire aboard. A full belly tank of gas jarred off one of our planes as he landed on deck. The tank burst and poured flaming gasoline all over the afterend of the flight deck. In less time than it takes to tell about it a huge pillar of flame and smoke enveloped the whole stern of the ship. Our escort destroyers thought we were finished, and stood by to pick up survivors; but we got the fire out quickly because most of the gas poured down the scuppers and over the side.

The only casualties were three lads seated in the head just below the flight deck, reading magazines when they should have been on deck. Some of the flaming gasoline came down the drain into the flushing system and my three studious sailors came out of the head like bats out of hell, hauling their pants up as they ran. The boys got little sympathy for their scorched fannies. By the time the chief boatswain's mate got through chewing them out for shirking, their ears were scorched, too.

Hunting subs around the Azores involved one job that seemed almost sacrilegious to me. In that part of the world you still see a few majestic old full-rigged sailing ships plying their way through the Trade Wind belts. To steam with one of these gracious old ladies within your horizon for an hour or so is a refreshing experience. It does things to your imagination. Even though you know that you belong to a less hardy generation of sailors, it makes you feel that you are a direct descendant of adventurous seafaring ancestors.

But these respectable looking old gals *could be* treacherous trollops. They would be ideal fronts for submarine refueling operations. So we gave them a thorough casing whenever we overhauled them although it always seemed to me to be just a little bit like suspecting your grandmother of robbing poor boxes.

One of these sailing ships gave our air groups a very humiliating twenty-four hours. An early morning patrol flight sighted a full-rigged three master about a hundred miles ahead of us. But when I told the next flight to get me further details on her they couldn't find her. I really threw the harpoon into those aviators who let a sailing ship get away from them. But this just shows that finding a moving ship at sea isn't as simple as some of our air-power enthusiasts make it seem when they are "proving" that carriers are sitting ducks for shore-based bombers. The ocean is a very big place; visibility at sea varies trickily, and shifting winds plus errors in aerial navigation sometimes will enable a five-knot sailing ship to give the slip to a 300 m.p.h. plane.

In the early days of naval aviation my scouting squadron often lost the *Saratoga,* at that time the biggest naval vessel in the world. Of course this usually resulted from the *Sara*'s habit of telling us that she was going to steam east while we were off on our search problem, and then changing her mind and running west as soon as we disappeared over the horizon. Actually, we didn't lose the ship —she lost *us*. Those dopey characters on the *Saratoga* seldom bothered to inform us about this little deviation from the agreed plan, and so we sometimes had a "bad time" getting back aboard, even though we had taken off from her only two hours before. The enemy doesn't tell you anything about his proposed movements or position in wartime.

But I had some caustic comments to make about it when this happened to us. The boys began to think they were looking for the *Flying Dutchman* before they finally found that sailing ship again. They have blamed my communicators ever since for decoding the initial sighting report improperly, and sending the subsequent flights out to a false position to start their search. . . . H'mmm.

Skippers of ships are subject to the same foibles as anyone else, and respond to digs at their pride the same way as human beings do ashore. One day we were operating about 150 miles south of a classmate of mine who commanded one of our rivals in the baby flattop league. The weather was fair where we were and we had our planes out, but it was on the ragged edge in his area, and evidently he had decided to wait a few hours until the sun burned some of the stuff off before launching his planes.

A pair of my boys patrolling to the north encountered the low-flying soup near the end of their leg and knowing it was clear behind them plowed in through the stuff for twenty miles or so, finding our rival ship with all planes on deck. They said nothing; simply circled the task group a couple of times, close enough for their markings to be identified and then headed back for the *Guadalcanal*. Upon return they reported that before they had completed their second circle our rivals had started launching planes.

I know exactly what went on on the bridge of that ship just as well as if I had been there. My classmate, his air group commander, and the aerologist, had their heads together sizing up the situation and weighing all the factors

166

involved very logically, until our planes arrived. Then my friend announced, perhaps not out loud, but at least to himself, "If that guy Gallery can fly in this stuff, so can we. . . . Launch aircraft."

A few days later we met a British convoy of about seventy ships bound for Gibraltar. The convoy knew that only the Allies had CVE task groups at sea; I knew the Germans didn't have any seventy ship convoys at sea, and we both had been advised to be on the lookout for each other. Nevertheless, we gravely went through the motions of challenging each other and exchanging recognition signals.

It was like a couple of small boys playing war, and all my signalmen and communicators entered into the game zestfully to determine promptly and infallibly for me whether this armada coming up over the horizon was friend or foe. They were especially anxious to do this because they were in the doghouse at this time, because I could read blinker messages better than our rookie sig- nalmen could. I was constantly getting in their hair when they requested repeats on words which they had missed in blinker messages from other ships. Having kibitzed on the transmission, I would supply the missing words plus a lot of salty comments on stupid signal floozies who couldn't read blinker. So they all welcomed this chance to redeem themselves.

But something was wrong. The goddam British wouldn't answer our challenges properly, and they wouldn't accept the answers we sent to their challenges, The signal bridges blinked back and forth at each other with their shielded searchlights, and the communicators fumbled through code books and diddled around verifying authenticators while we steamed past each other and disappeared below our respective horizons. Late that night my communication officer came up to the cabin with a very red face and confessed that we had missed a broadcast a few days before which had changed the recognition signals.

My British friend made an official report to the Commander in Chief, Mediterranean, when he arrived in Gibraltar. This immediately made the incident international high-level stuff.

Commander in Chief, Mediterranean, reported it to the Admiralty, who reported it to Washington, who asked the Commander in Chief, Atlantic Fleet, about it, who finally got me up on the carpet a month later. In just one word he asked me the question that always reduces a skipper's ego to the size of an ordinary seaman's—"Why?"

Shortly after the meeting with the convoy we pulled into Casablanca to refuel and have a couple of days liberty in this famous place. The first night four of our flyers went ashore to bend one on, after our hard voyage across the Atlantic, and, as sometimes happens when the boys are relaxing, things got a little bit mixed up.

Early in the evening one of their number passed out. His shipmates lugged the body around to the leading hotel, hired a room, and put their exhausted friend to bed so they could continue their explorations of the town. However, they had heard that not everybody in Casablanca was strictly trustworthy, so in order to protect their friend against robbery while in his helpless condition, they removed his wallet, watch, and cuff links and pocketed them for safekeeping. Then they left word at the desk to call him at 0700 and set off in search of further adventure.

The Arab bellboy had been present while all this was going on, and as soon as the other three left, he reported to the hotel manager that the American guest had been robbed by the three strangers who brought him in. The manager was just about to call the police when some other people from the ship arrived at the hotel, in somewhat better shape than the previous group. So the manager reported to them that one of their shipmates had been given knockout drops by a group of strangers, who had robbed him and left him in the hotel. The second group investigated and found the facts apparently as stated by the manager. Their shipmate was in a deep coma, minus all valuables. They indignantly reported the whole affair to the police headquarters, hauled their friend back to the ship, and turned him into his own bunk.

Next morning the three aviators slept till about noon. When they did get up, they were a bit fuzzy about some of the details of the previous evening and had forgotten all about parking their friend at the hotel. But meantime everybody else on the ship had heard about the robbery and were burned up about it—especially the victim.

Shortly after noon the chief of the local gendarmerie came aboard accompanied by the Arab bellboy. The first person the Arab spotted when he got on deck was one of the trio who had brought the body in. There was a great deal of shouting, gesticulating, and interpreting—and the thief was identified and accused.

The hung-over aviator hotly denied the accusation, but, reaching into his pocket for a handkerchief, he pulled out his friend's wallet. Then the fog began to lift and he remembered.

We finally pacified the Arab and the law and sent them ashore again. But you can hardly blame some of those ignorant foreigners if they think Americans are funny people.

On the way home from that cruise our flight deck crew learned how to fish wrecks out of catwalks. We had a damaged Avenger which we shoved over the edge of the flight deck and into the catwalk four or five times a day in every conceivable manner, then hauled it back on deck and shoved it over again.

Day after day my farm hands learned how to throw up sheer legs, clap a four-fold purchase on a sling around a plane's belly, lead the hauling part through a snatch block, set taut and run away with it in a manner that would have won admiration from John Paul Jones' seamen. By the time we got home they could whip any kind of a wreck out of the walkway, and have the landing area clear again in two and a half minutes by the stop watch, give or take a few seconds, depending on what the pay-master served for lunch that day.

After several days of this drill the boys were pretty well fed up with it, and really put their backs into it when they ran that plane off the deck, hoping to get up enough speed to bounce it clear over the side, and thus throw the damned thing plumb away. But it was like the Ancient Mariner's Albatross—they were stuck with it for the rest of the voyage.

One morning when we were about halfway home, just after sunrise, our lookout spied tall masts beyond the ocean's rim, dead ahead. Soon the biggest ship in the world hove up over the horizon on an opposite course, clipping along at thirty knots. A graceful 90,000-ton giant like the *Queen Elizabeth* does just as much to your imagination as one of those gracious old sailing ships, so we passed the word for all hands to lay up on deck and watch this majestic queen of the seas speed by. As she drew up broad off our starboard bow one of our planes, forty miles astern of us, radioed, "Sighted periscope, have submarine screw noises on sonobuoy,"

That busted up the lawn party like the proverbial skunk. We swung into the wind, banged off a killer group of planes, and cracked out a warning to the *Queen*. We worked that contact all day long but nothing more came of it. Just between you and me, I think our flyer saw a porpoise and heard the *Queen Elizabeth*. But officially, of course, we still claim that our vigilance and timely action averted the greatest maritime disaster in naval history.

Did I say we had *one* damaged Avenger on the way home? By the time we got home we had a hangar deck full of them. By working night and day Dick Kane's maintenance crews managed to keep six Avengers in flyable condition until just after we saved the *Queen Elizabeth*. We nursed those planes between flights like seconds work over their fighter between rounds. Then one day at noon when five TBM's were parked forward of the barrier, the last one of our morning flight made a bad land-

170

ing, bounced clear over the barrier, and landed smack in the middle of our last five flyable planes. Nobody got hurt, but there was blood, guts and feathers—of the airplane variety—all over the flight deck. That was the end of operations for that cruise.

CHAPTER 9

SKULDUGGERY ON THE
HIGH SEAS

Beginning with our next cruise in March, 1944, we tackled the problem of night flying. This was literally a plunge into the dark, because nobody had yet conducted night operations as a routine matter from a jeep carrier.

By this time the subs had found out that it wasn't safe to surface anywhere in the Atlantic in daylight. But they could still come up at night, beyond the range of shore-based aircraft, to recharge batteries and get a breath of fresh air.

We figured that by flying all night we could cash in on this situation as the *Card* and *Bogue* had on the earlier one. This may sound very simple when you read it now. But before we could do it we had to convert our flyers from fair weather pilots into night owls. Like breaking ice on any new field, this requires sweating a bit of blood while you are doing it. We sweated the necessary amount of blood without spilling any, in the first ten days of the cruise, learning how to operate at night, but it was hair-raising work at first.

I'm afraid I was more jittery than anyone else in the ship during these exploratory operations. Naval aviation, when I was growing up in it, had been a daytime outfit. There was no such thing as instrument flying in the early days. For a long time we thought that the seat of your pants could tell you just as much about what your plane was doing as any gyroscope. If we got caught in soupy weather on a cross-country flight we fell back on the "Iron Compass," flying down close to the first railroad track we saw and following it until it led us to an airport;

or went into a tunnel, in which case you just did the best you could.

We did go through motions of flying from the carriers at night, by making a few landings every now and then when the moon was full and conditions were exactly right. But this was a very special event. We didn't mind taking off a little before the crack of dawn, when we knew it would be daylight by the time we had to land. But we always tried to get the last plane of the afternoon flight back on board before sunset.

With twenty years of that tradition behind me, it was, in some ways, harder for me to become adapted to the idea of flying all night than it was for the youngsters, who were actually sticking their necks out, but who hadn't been brought up in the old school.

Occasionally our night operations on the *Guadalcanal* did get us into bad situations. Once on a black night an Avenger pilot made a bad approach; he floated over most of the arresting gear and then gave her the gun to go around again. He was too far over to starboard, so he hit the bridge with his wing, and wound up in a heap of flaming junk jammed against the island. Father Weldon, Bikkers and I were leaning over the edge of the bridge watching, and the impact occurred practically at our feet.

The crash threw gasoline all over the place and within a few seconds the little island was enveloped in smoke and flames. By one of those miracles that frequently happen on flight decks, all three of our boys in the plane scrambled out with only minor injuries. But there were four live depth charges left in the burning wreckage.

Your first impulse when you find yourself in a situation of this kind is, "Let's get the hell out of here until things cool off a bit."

However, we couldn't get out. The crash had blocked the only exit from the island structure. The only "out" for the three of us, and for about six others on watch on the bridge, was over the starboard side and into the water.

But if anybody suggests that you jump overboard on a

dark night in the middle of the Atlantic, you probably will say, "Let's not be too hasty about this proposition—let's wait awhile and see what happens."

We knew that if those depth charges behaved the way the Navy Department claimed they would, they could stand a hot gasoline fire for about three minutes before blowing up. So we braced ourselves, breathed as little smoke as we could, and stood by for further developments. In about two and one-half minutes our flight deck crew got the fire put out, and heaved the depth charges overboard. The day after that episode we took a page from the book of the wooden seashore hotels and rigged rope fire escapes at various strategic points around the bridge.

There is a sequel to this story. A year later while on duty in the Navy Department, I received a letter from the Chief Petty Officer who was in charge of the fire fighting parties on deck that night. He informed me that he was then on shore duty at a naval air station, had just been convicted by a summary court martial on charges of stealing five gallons of government gasoline, and had been sentenced to reduction in rating and loss of pay. His closing paragraph, although not quite as blunt as this, in effect said:

"Now, Captain, I took the heat off you one night about a year ago out in the Atlantic; what are you going to do about taking the heat off me now?"

I made a beeline for the Judge Advocate General's Office where I had a classmate on duty in a key spot, and we dug up the records of the case. It was immediately obvious to both of us that a grave injustice had been done and that my friend's constitutional rights had been outrageously violated. We chilled that rap in short order.

To get back to the start of our second cruise, breaking our group in at night flying was quite a gamble. We wrecked about one-third of our planes doing it, but so long as the boys were able to scramble out of the wrecks unhurt, I figured we would come out way ahead in the long run. It worked out that we arrived at the hunting grounds with only two-thirds of our planes left, but this smaller number of planes flying continuously around the clock, were at least twice as effective in catching submarines as our full group would have been flying only in the daylight. It was one of those gambles which make you look very foolish if they don't succeed, but to which you smugly refer after they have succeeded as a "calculated risk."

Actually this term, which has become very popular among military strategists, is just Pentagon gobbledegook for "taking a gamble." After calculating all the odds, as best you can sometimes you still don't know the answer, so you have a shot at it and hope for the best. You often have to do this in war, but it sounds a lot more scientific and impressive, when you write up the report of the operation, to call it a calculated risk after Lady Luck has pulled the fat out of the fire for you. You can't expect your flyers to stick their necks out willingly on a new and unproved operating technique unless you were willing to stick your neck out, too. If you want to fly at night, you've got to show enough lights to give your boys a reasonable chance in landing. You can't possibly shield those lights completely, so maybe a submarine will see your lights and torpedo you. The calculated risk enters here again. The best defense is a good offense, and we figured we were a lot safer at night with our planes in the air and showing a few lights, than we would have been with the ship darkened and all planes on deck.

One big reason why we were able to get away with this gamble was "Stretch" Jennings, our Landing Signal Officer. I say "big" advisedly because "Stretch" was a six-footer, and he used to practically stretch out from his signal platform on deck and get hold of the stick in airplanes coming up the groove whenever this became necessary.

The L.S.O. has one of the most important jobs on a carrier, because he actually flies every plane in to a landing.

His signals are not advisory, they are direct orders to the pilot and must be obeyed instantly whether the pilot agrees with them or not. At times it takes some frantic flag waving to get an erratic pilot aboard safely.

But when we were landing airplanes on a dark night with a lot of motion on the ship, "Stretch" was the calmest and most deliberate man on board. He wore a throat microphone so he could talk to the pilots as well as signal to them with his neon wands. I'm certain that "Stretch" could talk a bird down out of a tree, because I've often seen him do just about that on the *Guadalcanal.*

When "Stretch" was bringing you in he sounded like a mother singing a lullaby. His tone of voice inspired confidence. Everything was lovely all the way up the groove: "Bring your nose up just a little bit. . . . Just a little more . . . Just a touch more . . . *That's it.* . . . Now, cut." Pilots hit the deck thinking, "Boy, this is easy for a hotshot like me."

But then "Stretch" would storm into the pilot's ready room with fire blazing from his eyes and blast that pilot's hide off for being such a stupid cluck as to get his nose low in the first place, and for stubbornly refusing to pull it up after he had been told about it. These diatribes were masterpieces of profane, obscene and abusive language, and it was difficult to believe that they came from the same lips as those soothing lullabies in the groove. Everybody who ever landed on the *Guadalcanal* loved that big guy—and so did I.

We had a fine full moon when we started night flying so the boys began under easy conditions. Each night as they got more practice and improved in confidence and skill, the moon got a little smaller. By the end of two weeks when it had vanished altogether, the boys were able to bring their planes down nicely in total darkness.

From this time on we adjusted our ship's routine to cater to the moon. To get the fewest possible number of pitch-black take-offs and landings, we would vary our schedule according to the time of moonrise or moonset.

Since the time of these events changes by forty-five minutes every day, our schedule was constantly changing and every night's routine was different from the one before.

Churchill, in his memoirs referring to the changes in clock time when flying across the Atlantic which sometimes upset his meal hours, said, "One must not allow the sun to meddle in one's affairs." If Mr. Churchill had ever commanded a jeep carrier during night operations I think he would be more tolerant of the moon.

I became much better acquainted with the moon during this period than I had ever been before. Up to that time Mr. Moon had been just a casual acquaintance, whom I had gotten used to seeing around; a sort of an aloof and dreamy character giving off an anemic light which was of no practical value. But now he became an intimate friend whose appearance was anxiously awaited, and whom I greeted with a broad grin as soon as he showed his face over the horizon. Even a little sliver of a moon is a big help when you are flying from a jeep carrier, and a great big full moon, flooding the night with his abundant brilliance, is a glorious thing, giving you all the light you have any right to ask for. The good old moon is a lifelong pal of mine now.

It's customary for the skipper to be on the bridge whenever flight operations are in progress. However when you fly around the clock for weeks on end he can't do it. I used to turn in at sunrise every morning and sleep till noon, during which time my executive officer, Jesse Johnson, ran the task group. He ran it so well that one time he was able to wake me up with the news: "We've sunk another sub while you were asleep."

It didn't take long after we got to the hunting grounds to cash in on the night flying. Shortly after arrival off the Azores, about 10:00 P.M. on the night of April 8, one of our planes in VC-53, commanded by Lieutenant Commander Dick Gould, caught the *U-515,* outward bound from Lorient. She was fully surfaced and relaxing after the dangerous passage out from the Bay of Biscay.

Swooping down as low as he dared in the darkness, our plane plunked his load of depth charges close to the target—but not close enough to do serious damage. The salvo of "ash-cans" shook the U-boat up, sent the crew tumbling below, and forced the skipper to crash dive. But this gave us a confirmed and certain contact within sixty miles of the ship, so all we had to do was keep scouring the area until he had to come up again. We dispatched two of our four destroyers for the spot at full speed and kept the air full of planes all night.

The Captain of the *U-515*, with typical German stubbornness, was reluctant to believe that this far out from the Bay of Biscay he couldn't run on the surface at night as he always had in the past. He came up several times, but each time he did, he got a lot of stuff thrown at him from the air and had to duck again immediately. The best our boys could do in the darkness was to jar his ribs with near misses. But whenever this happened our speeding destroyers got new fixes on him from the planes, and shortly after sunrise they picked him up with their echo sounding gear.

The German turned out to be a tough customer. He knew every trick of the trade and he used them all on us. From sunrise till two that afternoon he stayed down at five hundred feet and led us through a tense and boisterous game of blind-man's buff, twisting, turning and doubling back on his tracks. In this game, when you finally grope into each other, one or the other of you is out and doesn't get to play any more. We shook our playmate up badly several times but we couldn't finish him off. A skillful sub skipper can do a lot of backing and filling in the time it takes depth charges to sink five hundred feet.

But even a veteran U-boat crew must have many things racing through their minds when the skipper is dodging and squirming with all their lives at stake. They think in silence, because the contestants in this duel are blind, and the battle is fought entirely by ear.

Water is an excellent conductor of sound, and both

178

the U-boat and her pursuers have listening devices which pick up the slightest sound and amplify it many times. Even a coffee cup dropped on the floor plate of a submerged sub may be heard by an alert destroyer prowling above. A noisy oil pump will blare out in a destroyer's ear phones like a fire alarm bell.

The sub's best chance to shake off her tormentors is to go deep and be as quiet as a mouse. Inside the one hundred-fathom curve she can sit on the bottom with everything stopped and the crew walking on tiptoe. But in the open sea the best she can do is put her back to the wall by going down to pressure depth, and creeping around as slowly and quietly as possible. She can't stop everything because you can never keep your boat in exactly neutral buoyancy. She is always either a little heavy or a little light, and you've got to keep moving to control your depth.

The crew of a sub trying to slink away in the depths can hear the propellers of approaching destroyers, can count the revolutions, and note the increase in volume as they come closer. They don't hear the supersonic *ping* which guides the groping destroyers to the firing point, but they do hear the Y guns when they fire the depth charge pattern, and they hear the charges hit the water. While those charges are sinking to the depth set on the hydrostats, the U-boat sailors are on the threshold of eternity. It must seem like hours before the charges go off, and the sub's hull is slugged by huge sledge hammer blows. That's the Old Man with a scythe over his shoulder knocking on the hull—though he pounds like a lusty young giant. But a depth charge must be very close to split a sub's sturdy pressure hull. It can smash lights and knock everybody off their feet without doing serious damage—if you omit the crew's morale from your estimates of damage.

Whenever depth charges come anywhere close to a sub, you can expect oil and wreckage to come to the surface. A sub deliberately spews out oil and rubbish whenever you get a near miss, hoping her tormentors will pick up a little sample of oil plus one or two pieces of junk and go hurrying home to claim an absolutely certain kill. They also turn loose noisemakers that float slowly to the surface and fill your ear phones with a deafening static. They eject chemicals, called "pillenwerfers," into their wake, thus making little air bubbles and giving the sonar operators a false target echo.

A cornered sub faces a grim dilemma in selecting the depth at which she will make her move to escape. If she stays near the surface, she is easier to find and to hit, but she is under less water pressure, and, if holed, she may be able to blow her tanks and get to the surface long enough for her crew to scramble out of the escape hatches before she goes down.

If she goes deep she has a little better chance of shaking her pursuers, but she loads her hull with hundreds of pounds per square inch of water pressure. A mere tap from a distant depth charge may crack her shell. If you are deep when a fatal wound is opened you may not have time to get to the surface again. The water may pour into the pressure hull faster than you can blow it out of your ballast tanks. If you lose this race between the incoming and ejected water, then you go down, down, down, until the pressure squeezes you flat, like a beer can full of flies that gets run over by a truck.

When this happens the people on the surface get no indication unless the lengthy reverberations of the depth charges have subsided, so they can hear the final *crunch* when the pressure hull collapses. Several hours later the first oil bubble may reach the surface and for a day or two there will be a growing slick at that spot on the ocean. Then all visible evidence of that U-boat and the sixty human beings who lived in her is gone forever.

At first I circled the scene of our battle with the *U-515* at a respectful distance in the *Guadalcanal,* with my two remaining destroyer escorts apprehensively patrolling around the carrier. Just before pipedown for lunch, one of these escorts sheared out at high speed, flying the signal which meant that she too had a sound contact. There was no use saving that last escort for the Junior prom, so I told him to hop on the new contact too, and I spent the next couple of hours, naked as a stripper at the end of her act, zig-zagging frantically in all directions. I made up several pretty good stories to tell the court-martial in case we got plunked while running around in this exposed condition.

Meantime our other two destroyers were tightening the noose around the *U-515*, and the depth charge patterns were getting closer and closer. At 1410 a well-placed salvo from the *Pope* jarred every frame in her hull, split her seams, and the jig was up. The sub blew all tanks, won the race against the incoming water, and suddenly broached to right between the *Pope* and the *Flaherty*. Hatches popped open and Nazis dove over the side while our destroyer escorts and planes blasted away with everything in their shot lockers. At 1414 the *U-515* heaved her bow straight in the air and sank stern first.

While the U-boat was upending herself like a sounding whale Commander Johnson yelled at the spellbound crowd on our flight deck: "Thar she blows—and sparm at that!"

We fished forty-four Nazis out of the water, and passed the word for the painter to lay up to the bridge on the double, to add another Nazi flag to our collection.

We got a beautiful set of pictures of the *U-515*, with one-third of her hull out of water pointing straight at the sky. I submitted these to the Assessment Board in Washington with the facetiously modest claim of "probably damaged."

Since our other two destroyer escorts had lost their contact, we reformed the task group. The same treatment, which had proved effective in the case of the *U-515*, seemed to be indicated for our second customer. So we kept combing the slowly expanding circle, centered on the noon contact, which contained all possible positions of the other sub.

Our submerged Nazi must have heard the ominous rumblings from depth charge explosions while the rhubarb with the *U-515* was going on, and he apparently concluded that the people causing this racket were unfriendly. At any rate, he didn't stick his head up until after midnight; then he yanked it right back down again just in time to keep from getting it knocked off. Continuous aerial patrols kept him down all night, but he couldn't hold his breath forever.

As the first light of dawn was tinting the eastern sky, he had to surface to give his battery a shot in the arm and to grab a couple of breaths of air. A few minutes after he came up, three of our planes ganged up on him fifty miles from the ship, bored in through the hail of AA fire which he sent up, and blasted his seams wide open.

Our planes came in at him from the dark western half of the sky and he never saw them until they opened up on him. It was too late to submerge then. He had to stay up and fight back like a cornered rat. Our rockets, machine gun bullets and depth charges ripped up the water and smashed through his hull. Another submarine crew learned in their last moments what "unrestricted submarine warfare" is like if you are on the receiving end. When the sun came up it found three dazed Nazis paddling around a litter of oil-soaked rubbish that marked the end of the trail for their U-boat.

We routed our hard-working painter out of his bunk again to put a fourth little swastika flag on our bridge.

The planes dropped life jackets to the three survivors left swimming in the water, and we ran over there at full speed to pick them up, keeping air spotters over them for the next three hours. There was only one man alive when we got there. Kastrup was his name. He was hanging onto a life jacket with one hand, and though badly hurt himself, held up a dead shipmate with the other.

We hauled them both out of the water and took Kastrup down to sick bay. We had the sailmaker sew his friend up in canvas with a five-inch shell at his feet and gave him a decent burial. They were from the *U-68,* one of the veterans of the U-boat fleet.

I had to do a nasty job that night while we were nailing the *U-68*. The weather was marginal at best, but I sent the boys out even though it was obvious they were not too enthusiastic about going. One of the lads got scared just as he rolled off the bow and into the inky darkness. He immediately started yelling on the radio to be taken back aboard again. When we asked him what was wrong all he would say was "the weather." The weather was just as bad for the three other planes in the flight as it was for him, but they were not complaining. If we brought one plane aboard on account of weather we should bring the others in, too.

A lot depended on getting the right precedents established in this night flying business, and what we did this night with a known submarine nearby would definitely establish one of them. If we admitted this weather was too bad to fly it meant that our planes would be on deck most of the time from then on. On the other hand, when a man says he doesn't like the setup, wants to land, and you refuse to let him, you are going to have trouble living with yourself from then on if he spins in and gets hurt. If he had given me any sort of an "out," such as claiming that his engine was running rough, I would have landed him immediately. But he didn't do that, so I left him up there circling close to the ship for four long black hours. Lady Luck was with me that time, because we eventually got my nervous lad aboard all in one piece, and the job that the other planes had done on the *U-68* proved that I had guessed right in refusing to listen to him.

The kid actually was out beyond his depth that night, and, through no fault of his own, wasn't ready for that kind of flying. But sometimes you have to give an individual a pretty lousy deal in order to get on with the war.

Admiral Ingersoll sent us one of those coveted "Well done" signals for the *U-515* job. His reply to our second dispatch, striking the *U-68* from the list of active public enemies, was an unprecedented "Exceptionally well done!" We were beginning to live up to that name on our stern!

During these operations a shore-based Liberator from the Azores missed the opportunity of a lifetime. He stumbled over us about midnight and apparently was quite surprised to find us flying at that time of night, because he circled us for half an hour while we landed one group of planes and launched another. All this time we were trying frantically to call him on every radio frequency he was supposed to guard, to ask his help in knocking off the *U-515*. He had the equipment to do an efficient job in the dark. Our planes didn't, but we couldn't raise him.

As our pair of planes headed for the latest fix on the *U-515,* he flew up and sniffed curiously at their tails for about ten miles and then buzzed off on his assigned mission, whatever that was. He would probably have another star in his air medal now if he had been tuned in on the right radio program.

After disposing of *U-68,* we had time to devote some attention to the survivors of the *U-515*. We called the destroyers alongside, rigged a breeches buoy, and transferred the four officers and forty men of the submarine to the *Guadalcanal*.

It turned out that we had made an important haul. Her skipper was Kapitan Leutnant Werner Henke, Knight's Cross of the Iron Cross with Oak Leaves, one of the aces of the U-boat fleet, with 150,000 tons of Allied shipping to his credit. He was a Junker, a clean-cut looking fellow, professional regular navy man, but somewhat on the arrogant side. He greeted me with an indignant protest that I had killed six of his men after he had come up to surrender!

His men respected his ability as a U-boat skipper but they didn't like him. They said he took unnecessary chances and they blamed the loss of the *U-515* on his reckless confidence that he would sink us before we could get him. His men were also bitter toward him because he had frozen promotion for two years among his hand-picked crew, to prevent any of them from being transferred to other U-boats if they were advanced in rank.

184

I also learned from his crew that in addition to being a very able fellow, he was an ambitious one. He had been eligible for shore duty in January, 1944, but had begged permission to make one more cruise in the *U-515* in order to sink the additional tonnage he needed in order to add diamonds to the Oak Leaves in his Iron Cross. As it turned out, eventually, he exchanged his Iron Cross for a simple wooden one.

In his dealings with me Henke's attitude was formal, respectful, and "correct." But, as will appear presently, by being a bit stuffy about his rights as a prisoner of war, he got himself taken for quite a sleigh ride.

I believe that according to the storybook writers, you are supposed to invite a captured skipper up to the cabin for dinner. I don't know what Emily Post will say about this, but I took no stock in that idea. For one thing, it was bound to be embarrassing for the guest because he certainly couldn't return my hospitality.

I put Kapitan Henke and his officers in the brig, put all the petty officers in the forward uptake compartment, and the non-rated men in the after uptakes. We kept these three distinct groups of Germans isolated from each other all the time we had them aboard so they couldn't give each other any pep talks, or hatch any plots against the United States or the *Guadalcanal*, especially the *Guadalcanal*.

Henke's Junker instincts soon rebelled at the idea of living in the brig—and thereby hangs a tale.

The day after we took the prisoners aboard, Henke sent word up from the brig that he would like to see me, so I had him brought up to the cabin. He spoke English perfectly, and respectfully invited my attention to the Geneva Convention, put in a beef about being quartered in the ship's prison, and stated that according to the laws of war, he was entitled to an officer's stateroom.

I didn't have my copy of the laws of war handy but I explained to Henke that the ship was crowded and that it was entirely impracticable to grant his demand. I also told him that we had many lads on board of Polish and Jewish descent and that I was afraid some of them might not be very nice to him if we gave him the freedom of the ship.

Then, just as a shot in the dark, I added that we were scheduled to refuel at Gibraltar in a few days and that if he was not satisfied with the treatment I was giving him, I could arrange to turn him and his crew over to the British there, if he so desired. This statement was not entirely true in all respects. In the first place, we were not going anywhere near Gibraltar; in the second place, if we had gone there, the whole British Mediterranean Fleet couldn't have taken those prisoners from me. We were bringing them home for *proof* this time to the skeptics in Washington.

However, my suggestion produced an immediate change in Henke's attitude. He assured me that conditions in the brig were not so bad as to require any such drastic action, and that he would be able to put up with them until we reached the United States.

Several days later my Chief Master at Arms, who brought Henke his food and who had gotten on fairly good terms with him, came to me with a very interesting story, obtained through casual conversation with Henke. Just before the *U-515* sailed on this cruise (according to Henke), a British propaganda broadcast, beamed at the U-boat bases in France, carried the announcement that the British knew it was the *U-515* which had sunk the *Ceramic* with the loss of several thousand lives in 1942. This broadcast went on to say that the British had found out that, after the sinking, the *U-515* surfaced and machine-gunned the lifeboats filled with survivors. (Henke denied this.) The British then announced that if any of the crew of the *U-515* ever fell into their hands, they would be tried as pirates and hung if convicted.

After thinking this story over for a while, I decided to see just how far I could push the idea of turning Henke over to the British. I am as sure as you can ever be about a mortal enemy that Henke would not have machine-gunned a lifeboat. But, nevertheless, I had a message prepared, on a top secret dispatch blank, purporting to come from CinC Atlantic Fleet to the *Guadalcanal* saying:

Admiralty has requested that you turn survivors of *U-515* over to British authorities when you refuel in Gibraltar. In view of the crowded condition of your ship, you are authorized to use your discretion.

I also drew up the following statement on legal paper with the Ship's Seal on it, ready for signature by Henke:

"I, Kapitan Leutnant Henke, hereby promise on my honor as a German officer that if I and my crew are imprisoned in the U.S. instead of England, I will answer all questions truthfully when I am interrogated.

Signed_____
Kapitan Leutnant

_____

D.V. Gallery, Capt., USN

_____

J.S. Johnson, Comdr., USN

Sizing up all the angles before trying this shenanigan, it did not seem to me that the chance of success was very good. But it did seem that this was one of those situations where you have nothing to lose, and might possibly gain something. The worst that could happen would be for Henke to spit in my face and tell me to go to hell; which would not affect the outcome of the war one way or the other. On the other hand, if the idea worked, something pretty good might come of it.

Anyway, I decided to try this monkey business and see what happened. So I sent for a large-scale anchorage chart of Gibraltar and laid it out on the cabin table where Henke was bound to see it.

I got Commander Johnson up to the cabin to act as a witness; had the Chief Master at Arms bring Henke up from the brig; and handed him the phony dispatch. His face fell when he read it, and it was obvious that he took a dim view of the matter. After a long pause, he shrugged his shoulders and said, "Well, I suppose there is nothing to be done about it."

I replied, "Maybe there is. That dispatch authorizes me to use my discretion, and if you make it worth my while, I will keep you on board till we arrive in the United States."

"What do you want me to do?" asked Henke.

I then pushed the prepared statement across the table to him, laid the pen alongside it, and said, "Just sign this statement."

Henke read the paper through carefully several times, thought it over quite awhile and then said, "Captain, you know I can't sign that."

I replied, "It's entirely up to you. Sign, and you go to the United States—otherwise you go to England."

Henke finally said, "Well, Captain, what would *you* do if you were in my position?"

I replied, "If I were convinced that my country had lost the war, and that I could help my crew by signing it, I would sign."

Henke stood on the opposite side of the table for several minutes without saying a word. It was like a scene in a movie. Then he picked up the pen, signed the paper, and went back to the brig.

We then circulated the agreement which the skipper had signed, among the petty officers and non-rated men in the two prisoner compartments, and put a similar proposition to the entire crew. The agreements for the enlisted men went into considerably more detail than that signed by Henke, and embodied agreements to describe operational procedures and details of equipment.

U. S. S. GUADALCANAL

151325

#4

BRITISH AUTHORITIES REQUEST HENKE AND CREW OF U-515 BE TURNED

OVER TO THEM AT ~~~~~~~ X IN VIEW OF CROWDED CONDITION OF

YOUR SHIP YOU ARE AUTHORIZED TO USE YOUR DISCRETION..........

Phony message used to persuade crew of U-515 to sign agreement to talk.

SECRET

PRECEDENCE   PRIORITY

TD 1320
DATE 4/15/44

FM: CINC ATLANTIC FLEET

TO: USS GUADALCANAL

INFO:

Capt	Exec	OOD	Duty Com Off	Exec Off	Ship Sec	Com	Nav	Com	Eng	1st Lt	Sup	Disb	Med	Chap	Rdar	Air Aero	Air Plot	VCB	Date and Time GR
A																			151325
																			cwo JWD

Every man in the crew signed without hesitation, agreeing to tell all he knew.

Upon arrival in the United States Henke reneged on his agreement, as I felt sure he would, on the ground that it had been obtained under duress and false pretenses. But his crew never knew this. Apparently they all figured, "The skipper is talking, why shouldn't we?" So when interrogated by the anti-submarine warfare experts of the Navy Department they sang like canary birds, and the Office of Naval Intelligence made quite a haul.

Now that we have won the war, I have no doubt that some bubbleheaded people will say that I was guilty of using dishonorable tactics. However, I fed Henke well, gave him a comfortable bunk to sleep in, and used no rubber hose or drugs on him. When I think of Buchenwald I am able to roll over and go to sleep with a perfectly clear conscience.

When questioning prisoners, Dr. Monat was our official interpreter. On numerous occasions I shook my finger under his nose and told him that all I wanted to do was to translate what I said into German and what the prisoners said in English. He always assured me that he understood and would comply, but his Gallic temperament and background usually got the better of him. My questions were much too simple, and failed to drive home such important matters as war guilt, the evils of the Nazi ideology, etc.

When I asked a question requiring only a "yes" or "no" answer, Henry would launch into a torrent of German, gesticulating all over the place, reviewing the past ten years of German infamy, and denouncing Hitler and all his works and pomps. After a heated harangue of the prisoner, he would turn to me and report, "He says 'no.'"

You couldn't help respecting some of these German submariners. Most of them would reply to improper questions with the simple statement, "Ich bin deutscher soldaten." (I am a German soldier.)

I made one attempt to get information out of Kastrup,

sole survivor of the *U-68,* and got myself properly squelched in doing so. Kastrup and two men had been on lookout watch up on the conning tower when our planes attacked and wounded the other two men. Kastrup attempted to drag his wounded shipmates to the conning tower hatch and then get them below. But while he was doing this, the officer of the watch slammed the hatch shut and submerged the boat, leaving his three lookouts to swim for it in the middle of the Atlantic.

I thought I might get Kastrup to talk by playing up the idea that his skipper had deliberately abandoned him. He stopped that line of attack cold with the simple and obviously sincere statement: "It was the Captain's duty to sacrifice me and save his ship."

We even tried some storybook stuff, such as concealing microphones and recording devices in the prisoners' compartments. But it was no dice. All that got us was the names and telephone numbers of some red-hot babes in Cherbourg, Brest, and Kiel. Evidently our visitors were too fed up with life in the U-boat fleet to talk about it any more, and were quite happy to get out of it with their lives. Except for Henke and his crew, I was never able to get anything out of any of them but their names, ranks, and the number of their U-boat. Henke committed suicide after he found out how he had been used to make his crew talk.

A few days after we got the *U-515,* we had a plane go down in a rough sea 140 miles from the ship. His radio had gone out about 3:00 A.M. one very black night under a solid overcast and he was unable to find his way back to the ship. Groping around in the dark with nothing below you but a vast ocean of whitecaps, unable even to send an S.O.S., and with your gasoline gauge slowly approaching zero, is a grim way to have your time run out.

However, our lad kept his wits and climbed as high as his plane would go, hoping that we might "see" him on our radar, recognize his plight, and do something about it.

We did! We banged off another plane and vectored

him up through the overcast toward our stray chick. Despite the fact that we were in submarine waters, we turned on a big searchlight and pointed it up in the sky. I figured that this was the price you have to pay for operating planes at night, and if you weren't willing to pay it when one of the boys needed help then you had no right to send him out in the dark. But our lad was so far off his course he couldn't even see the searchlight.

It was impossible for our chase plane to actually make contact until after dawn, but for the last part of his ordeal, our wandering boy had a Guardian Angel hovering near and just waiting for the sun to come up so he could spot him, tap him on the shoulder, and lead him home. The wanderer ran out of gas as the sun peeked over the horizon and our shadow spotted him as he was going down through the clouds with a dead stick. He had hardly finished splashing when our plane zoomed over him and dropped a rubber boat to the three grateful boys in the water.

A destroyer was already on the way to the spot at full speed. Meanwhile, we kept a pair of planes over the spot, one down below freezing contact with that little raft among the whitecaps, and the other alternately climbing way up through the overcast where we could check his position on the radar, and then dropping down again to sight the plane over the raft.

All morning long we got a constant series of reports from our planes which we put on the ship's loudspeaker system and broadcast to our own crew. One message sent by hand signal from the raft and relayed by the circling plane was: "Tell *Guadalcanal* to be sure to save chow for us!"

They were safe and sound aboard the destroyer by noon and back on the *Guadalcanal* for dinner that night. When you give the boys that kind of service they feel that they really belong to the ship's company, and are a little happier about it when you send them out on a foul night, like a prize fight manager who pats his boy on the back and says, "Get in there and fight, son; that big bum can't hurt *us*."

Another time the alertness of one of our radar operators saved three boys who thought they "had had it." Their plane was launched on a black night and five minutes later the pilot called in to report he had tested all his equipment, everything was working, and he was shoving off on the first leg of his search. He had hardly finished making this report when one of the operators of the radar scope in C.I.C. noticed that the blip from that plane had disappeared from the scope.

The rest of us were inclined to shrug this off because we had been talking to the lad only half a minute before, and had just heard him say that everything was lovely. But our radar man was emphatic that the scope was O.K., and that something must have happened to that plane. So, reluctantly and somewhat apologetic about cluttering up the air, we made another test call to the plane. When we got no answer we vectored a destroyer out ten miles into the blackness, and at the exact spot which our radar man was marking on his scope, they fished our three boys out of the water.

Somehow or other that plane's altimeter had been set at one thousand feet instead of zero, when he was on deck. Right after reporting in to us, the pilot noticed he was two thousand feet by his altimeter, and started letting down to one thousand where he belonged. You can't tell by looking how far from the water you are on a black night, and just as his altimeter reached one thousand feet he smacked the ocean and found himself ten feet underwater. Even after he and his two crew members got out of the wreck and reached the surface, their outlook was grim. Their next radio report wasn't due for an hour and a half. By that time the task group would be thirty miles further away; the area necessary to be searched for a ditched plane would have grown to about one thousand square miles, and their chance for being rescued would have shrunk to almost zero. Lady Luck was with us again that night.

But we also had bad luck as well as good. One day we sent a plane out in the middle of the afternoon on a patrol that shouldn't have taken him more than a hundred miles from the ship. It was clear and unlimited that day and you could see forty miles. After he checked out on his first leg we never heard a word from him again. An hour later, after he failed to check in on time, we launched search planes, detached all our destroyers on a scouting line, made heavy smoke, and opened up on the radio.

He came down five hours later, one hundred yards offshore of Flores Island in the Azores, and five hundred miles from the ship. All three of the lads in the plane drowned, trying to swim ashore through the surf.

Impossible tragedies like that one, and miraculous rescues like those two at night, are the reasons why many aviators figure that we live until our number comes up.

On the way back to Norfolk with our prisoners from the *U-515* and *U-68* we had time to hash over our career to date. We had bagged four pelts on our first two cruises. Currently we led the league in the Battle of the Atlantic and were rapidly overhauling the records of the *Card,* the *Core,* and the *Bogue,* who had a year's head start on us. We certainly could not complain about the way Lady Luck was treating us.

But as we fought that battle with the *U-515* over and over again on the way home, an idea began to take shape in our minds. It seemed fantastic at first, but our luck was riding high; we called ourselves the "Can Do" ship, and on sober, second thought, the idea had possibilities.

Why not try to board and capture the next submarine we fetched up from the depths? After all, Henke was an ace of the U-boat fleet. The *U-515* had been one of Hitler's crack U-boats. She surfaced within hailing distance of three of our destroyers at point-blank torpedo range. But still, when brought to bay, *she didn't fight,* she didn't

194

blow herself up. Henke and his veteran crew, when cornered, had just one urge—to save their skins.

The tempting idea kept recurring, that if we had had sufficient imagination to foresee our opportunity, and to be set for it, we might have made naval history by boarding and capturing the *U-515*.

It's true that attempting to board and capture a sub would be dangerous business. We might get ourselves sunk by a cripple which was on its way to the bottom, but was still willing to fire its last torpedoes. However, you will never do much in a war unless you are willing to take some chances. The history books are full of incidents where naval commanders have missed golden opportunities because they worried too much about what the enemy *might* do to them instead of what they could do to the enemy. Witness Kurita at the Battle of San Bernardino Strait.

If we could capture a submarine and get her code books, it would be worth taking long chances. The Naval Communications Office in Washington could then set a watch on the Nazi submarine frequency and read their operational orders. This would be like sticking your head into the opponent's huddle in a football game. The Nazi radio operators at Naval H.Q. in Berlin would all become U.S. intelligence agents!

Coming back from that second cruise, we decided that our program for the third cruise would be to tow a U-boat home.

CHAPTER 10

AWAY BOARDERS!

At the departure conference of all skippers in the task group, just before shoving off on our third cruise, I outlined the plan for capture.

We agreed that the only reason why a submarine would surface while under attack was to allow the crew to escape from a damaged boat before scuttling it. So, there was no need for us to fire any lethal stuff at a sub after she surfaced, because the Nazis would pull the plug on it themselves. We therefore decided that on this cruise we would operate exactly as we had on the others except that as soon as a cornered sub came up, we would cease firing anything which could inflict further structural damage. We would endeavor to create panic and thus expedite the evacuation of the boat by the fire of small caliber automatic weapons, and would meantime try to get aboard ourselves in time to put the "plug" back in. We also decided that each ship in the task group would organize a boarding party and keep a whaleboat ready to lower in a hurry.

I'm sure that some of those who sat in on the conference had their tongues in their cheeks while we were discussing this plan. Observers from the staffs of Commander in Chief, Atlantic Fleet; Commander Air Force, Atlantic Fleet; and anti-submarine warfare experts from Washington always attended these departure conferences. I saw several of these kibitzers exchange knowing glances and make circular motions with the forefinger pointed at their heads while we were laying our plans for capture.

You could hardly blame them for being skeptical. The last time the U.S. Navy had boarded and captured a foreign enemy man-of-war in battle on the high seas had been in 1815, when the U.S.S. *Peacock* captured H.M.S. *Nautilus* in the Straits of Sunda. Some changes had occurred in naval tactics and weapons since then. We realized that we would need several remarkably lucky breaks to be able to do this job. We couldn't make these breaks, but we could be ready to cash in on them if we happened to get them. So we made our plans, visionary though they may have been, and agreed that our objective would be to bring a sub home on the end of a towline.

On our way to the hunting ground we checked our new squadron out as night flyers. Most of them had only recently earned their wings, so they belonged to the new generation of naval aviators who didn't know that you weren't supposed to fly at night from jeep carriers. They took to it like a bunch of owls.

While I was in the *Guadalcanal* we got three new squadrons which had never landed on a carrier at night, and in about ten nights broke them in to operate around the clock.

It was possible to do this because of the splendid basic training which our boys got at Pensacola. Even when we were converting college boys into aviators on a mass production basis, the Navy kept its standards high, and reaped rich rewards by doing so. Early in the war the Jap naval aviators were high-caliber pilots who gave us plenty of trouble before we killed most of them off. But the quality of the Jap replacements was low, and at the Mariana Turkey Shoot our new but well-trained pilots slaughtered them.

Right after we finished qualifying our pilots in the hazardous business of night flying without hurting anybody, one of our lads lost his life on a simple, routine, daylight flight, because of a fantastically improbable mistake.

One morning the pilot of an Avenger forgot to shift his gas valve from the port to the starboard tank until his port tank ran dry and the engine quit. This was nothing to get excited about; he simply flipped his valve to the starboard tank and in about thirty seconds the engine picked up again and he resumed his flight back to the ship. More as an afterthought than anything else he reported this by voice radio to the ship.

But during those thirty seconds a grim miscarriage occurred in the radio operating compartment behind the pilot's back. Since this flight was just a routine training mission, two inexperienced radio operators had been allowed to take the places of the regular crewmen.

Of course *everybody* knows that no one gets hurt in a water landing. But somehow or other these two men apparently didn't know it, and both got panicky when the engine quit.

One of them yelled, "Bail out," and did so himself. The other lad followed suit and either didn't pull his rip cord or maybe he was too low for his chute to open. The first man came down in the water safely and blew up his Mae West. The other lad plummeted down and didn't come up again.

All this happened without the pilot knowing a thing about it. On the ship we didn't find out that anything was wrong, until he landed aboard and we found the escape hatch of the after compartment open and the occupants missing.

We made a quick check on our radar plot of the plane's position twenty minutes previously when the pilot had said his engine cut out, and sent all planes back to search. Fortunately the sea was calm, our searchers spotted a green dye marker in the water, and an escort destroyer reached the spot and recovered one man a few hours later.

One of the morals of this story is that sometimes cutting red tape is dangerous. We had set up a system on the ship designed to prevent anyone from making a flight as an aircrewman until he had gone through a long rigmarole of instruction on a lot of things, some of which were pretty obvious. On this particular morning someone had cut the red tape and allowed two enthusiastic amateurs to go out on a flight before making certain that they knew the facts of life.

Soon after this we reached the hunting ground off the Azores and got down to business. This time it turned out to be tedious business. We flew around the clock day after day and night after night without even a false alarm for our efforts. We shifted our search and rooted around the Cape Verde Islands for a while, but had no better luck down there.

After three weeks of unsuccessful hunting, shortage of fuel necessitated starting for Casablanca. One submarine was suspected to be near our route to Casablanca, so we determined to hunt that one as long as fuel permitted.

Meanwhile my communicators decoded another one of those top secret messages from a task group several hundred miles from us, announcing that our sister ship, the *Block Island,* engaged on the same sort of duty, had just been torpedoed and sunk. I neglected to bawl out the watch officer who broke that one. Next morning I assembled the whole crew on the flight deck, made the announcement, and then asked, "Does this news scare us?" I allowed about fifteen seconds for the lads to think it over, and then went on to say, "I can see the answer in your faces, and the answer is, 'Hell, no!'" To tell the truth, the actual answer was, "You're damned right it does," and that went for me, too!

For the next few days and nights we combed the ocean with our planes chasing will-o'-the-wisps. We had briefly glimpsed visual sightings which were either periscopes or porpoises. We had disappearing ghosts on our radar scopes, we had noisy sonobuoys, and our radio direction finders picked up suspicious transmissions. We were sure that there were submarines near us but we couldn't flush them.

We found out later that we were getting unexpected help all the time from the stream of Army transport planes crossing this area enroute from South America to Africa. Every time the submarines popped up at night they saw an airplane on their radar scope, jumped to the conclusion that the airplane saw them, too, and crash dived. Sometimes they saw our planes and sometimes they saw the perfectly harmless Army transports, but they couldn't tell the difference. This was help for us in the sense that it forced the sub down and made him use up his battery.

On the morning of Sunday, June 4, we were a hundred miles off Cape Blanco, French West Africa, when the orderly brought me in a copy of the Plan of the Day. This is a routine daily mimeographed sheet, which sets forth the schedule for the day and contains notes and orders about the internal business of the ship. It is made up and printed the day before it is distributed. One section of the plan which the orderly handed me that morning was headed, "Crew For Captured Submarine." We had been canvassing our crew ever since leaving Norfolk to find people who knew something about storage batteries, Diesels, or anything else that might be useful to the prize crew of a submarine. Everybody wanted to be in this crew, and now the long list of claimants for places had finally been narrowed down to the twenty who were deemed to be best qualified—or, perhaps, least unqualified would be more accurate. I scanned this item on the Plan of the Day somewhat wryly and thought: "Maybe we'll have better luck on the return voyage."

We had stretched our fuel supply to its absolute limit by this time, in fact a little beyond, I think—but subsequent events spared me the acute embarrassment of having this become public knowledge. So we reluctantly abandoned the hunt and headed for Casablanca. I had just come up on the bridge after attending Mass when the radio loudspeaker announced: "U.S.S. *Chatelain* to Task Group Commander. I have a possible sound contact."

That was nothing startling. "Possible sound contacts" are made every day. However, our doctrine was to treat them all with respect. The *Guadalcanal* swung away from the contact and put on full speed, while the two nearest destroyers broke off to assist the *Chatelain*. A carrier right smack at the scene of a sound contact is like an old lady

n a barroom brawl. She has no business there, and can
do nothing but get in the way of those who are going to
need elbowroom for the work at hand.

So far, this was no different from any other doubtful
sound contacts. But, now, Lieutenant Commander D. S.
Knox, skipper of the *Chatelain,* reported, "Contact evaluated as sub. Am starting attack." He immediately dropped
his depth charges.

Our two Wildcat fighters which had streaked over to
the *Chatelain's* position, were just starting to circle overhead like hawks ready to pounce on their prey. As the
Chatelain's depth charges hit the water, both fighter pilots
sighted the long dark shape of the submarine running
fully submerged.

Ensign J. W. Cadle, flying one of the Wildcats, sang out
on the radio, "Sighted sub." Lieutenant W. W. Roberts,
in the other fighter, confirmed.

At this point the sub first spotted us and reversed course,
ramming her diving planes to the down position to shake
off the *Chatelain* and go deep. But the airplanes promptly
reported this to the *Chatelain,* advising her to reverse
course too, and fired their machine guns into the water
to indicate the spot where the sub was disappearing. The
Chatelain swung around, following the directions from the
air and the indications of her sound gear, and delivered
her Sunday punch of depth charges. This is one of the few
cases in which an aircraft actually directed the attack of a
surface vessel on a submarine.

By this time all eyes were on the *Chatelain.* Cheers
went up as the depth charges exploded. As the first depth-
charge plumes were subsiding, Ensign Cadle clamped
down the transmitter button in his plane and jubilantly
shouted, "You've struck oil! Sub is surfacing!" At 11:22½,
just twelve and a half minutes after the *Chatelain's* original
report, all doubt was dispelled. The sinister black hull of
a submarine hove itself up out of the water less than
seven hundred yards from the *Chatelain.* As she broke surface with depth-charge plumes still rising all around her,

the *Chatelain, Pillsbury* and *Jenks* opened fire with their small-caliber antiaircraft guns, and the two fighter planes cracked down on her, strafing her decks with their .50 caliber fixed machine guns. The *Guadalcanal, Pope* and *Flaherty* had itchy trigger fingers too, but held their fire because the other destroyers were in the way.

Hundreds of men lined the decks of our carrier and crowded to topside positions on the destroyers for ringside seats. The three destroyers firing on the U-boat formed a rough crescent around her and hammered streams of shrapnel shells into the U-boat's conning tower. From above, the Wildcats swooped down, their .50 caliber machine guns blazing and sending torrents of hot steel ripping across the sub's deck and ricocheting through her superstructure. All this gunfire was potentially lethal to personnel but was harmless so far as the pressure hull of the U-boat was concerned.

We found out later from the Nazis that their first warning of danger came when the *Chatelain's* depth-charge pattern shattered the peaceful noonday atmosphere by exploding all around them just as they sat down for Sunday dinner. The explosions smashed the lights, rolled the U-boat on her beam's end and dumped everybody into the bilges under a heap of mess tables, crockery and food. The panic-stricken Nazis scrambled out of the bilges and rushed for the conning tower escape hatch, yelling that the after torpedo room was blown wide open and that the boat was sinking.

The stunned skipper took their word for this, blew his tanks, surfaced, and gave the order to scuttle and abandon ship.

As the sub surfaced, it flashed through my mind, "Here is exactly the situation we were hoping for—this is where we came in on the *U-515!*" So I grabbed the mike on the bridge and broadcast, "I want to capture this bastard if possible."

Our crazy plan worked to perfection, and the Nazis performed as predicted. We plastered the U-boat with small stuff and the Germans went overboard so fast they didn't even stop the engines, but left the sub circling at eight knots! The ancient call, *"Away all boarding parties!"* boomed out for the first time over modern loudspeakers. Whaleboats plopped into the water and streaked for the sub. Lieutenant David from the *Pillsbury* leaped aboard the U-boat just after the last Nazi took his departure. As his whaleboat plunged alongside the circling sub and made fast for this historic Nantucket sleigh ride, I broadcast for the benefit of the task group: "Heigh ho, *Pillsbury*, ride 'em cowboy!" Not a very salty exhortation, but readily intelligible to all concerned.

There was no one on the sub's deck now except one dead German—miraculously, the only man on either side killed during the entire engagement. However, there was every reason to believe that there were still Nazis below, opening sea cocks and getting ready to blow up their vessel. The very fact that the sub was running at good speed, surfaced, seemed to indicate that she was not totally abandoned. But this didn't give David pause. Without hesitating, he and A. W. Knispel, torpedoman's mate, third class, and S. E. Wdowiak, radioman, second class, plunged down the conning tower hatch, ready to fight it out with any Krauts below.

As soon as they hit the floor plates, one ran aft and one ran forward with tommy guns, and found, to their amazement, that the boat was all theirs—all theirs, that is, if she didn't sink or blow up!

David and his party of eight laid their lives on the line when they boarded that U-boat. They had every reason to believe that they would be greeted by a blast of machine gun bullets when they started down the hatch. They also knew that all German subs were fitted with fourteen time-fused demolition charges, but they didn't know what time it was by the German's clocks. This made no difference to David and his boys.

David got the Congressional Medal of Honor for this job. Only one other was awarded in the Battle of the

Atlantic. His two principal helpers, Knispel and Wdowiak, should have gotten it too, but they had to settle for Navy Crosses.

The boarders found that the Nazi had done a hurried job of scuttling, and the sub was rapidly filling with water. As soon as our boys pulled the switches on the sub's main motors, she went down so far by the stern that they had to start the motors up again to keep headway and hold the stern up.

They also found that the sub wasn't as badly damaged as the Germans thought she was. As we found later, the damage was confined to her *external* ballast tanks, and the boat's pressure hull was intact.

The rest of the boarding party now were busy closing the valves which the Nazis had opened. In the main control room they found a stream of water six inches in diameter pouring into the hull, through a large strainer in a sea connection which had the cover knocked off, to make certain that the boat went down, even if all the other scuttling measures taken should fail. This stream of water would have sunk her in a few more minutes, but the boarders found the missing cover, slapped it back in place and stopped the water.

Boarding parties from the *Guadalcanal* were now swarming aboard. One party literally arrived with a bang when its boat was picked up by the sea and deposited bodily on the deck of the submarine. This crash caused some concern to the stouthearted lads from the *Pillsbury* who were busy down below and didn't know what was going on above. Only a few minutes earlier the sub had received a bad bump from the *Pillsbury* when she finally got alongside. This bump drove the submarine's port bow diving planes clear through the paper thin plates of the destroyer, and when the *Pillsbury* sheered out again, she wrenched off the diving planes. The *Pillsbury* was then obliged to haul clear with water pouring into her forward engine room and her sound room, both of which were soon flooded to the waterline.

As the *Pillsbury* limped clear of the arena she signaled to us that the submarine had to be towed to remain afloat. So the *Guadalcanal* signaled back, "Have submarine stop engines and we will take her in tow."

The crew of the *Guadalcanal* had been kept informed of each new development in the battle by the ship's public address system. Right after the electrifying announcement that we were taking the sub in tow ourselves a conscientious boatswain's mate on the bridge, carrying out the check-off list for routine daily announcements, boomed over the loudspeakers, "Now the name of the movie for tonight will be . . ." The raucous laughter that broke the tension drowned out the rest of the announcement.

When the sub stopped, she again settled with her stern down, coming to rest with about twenty feet of her bow and three feet of the conning tower remaining above water. We pulled alongside and put our stern close aboard the submarine's bow. The U-boat's ugly snout, with its four loaded torpedo tubes, was almost touching the side of our ship. I said a fervent prayer, "Dear Lord, I've got a bunch of inquisitive young lads on that submarine. Please don't let any of them monkey with the firing switch."

We lost no time passing a one-and-a-quarter-inch tow wire to our lads on the forecastle. Soon we were underway again with our prize in tow. As we gained headway the sub's stern came up again, reviving our hopes, which had been sinking as the sub settled lower in the water.

The boarding parties worked fast and furiously, disconnecting electric leads from demolition charges, looking for booby traps and passing up on deck all secret papers and documents, so that we would have something to show for it in case we still lost the U-boat.

The papers and documents removed at this time were of inestimable value. The crew had abandoned the sub so hastily, and were so sure she was going down, that they hadn't bothered to destroy anything. We thus got possession of every chart, publication, general order and code book that an operating submarine carries. From the point of view of Naval Intelligence it was the greatest windfall of the war.

One group of men, now in the task group, watched the proceedings with different emotions from ours. The *Chatelain* had picked up about forty survivors from the sub, and had herded them on her forecastle, where seamen armed with tommy guns kept them covered. They looked on grimly and silently from a distance of five hundred yards while we took their ship in tow.

Just before the *Pillsbury's* boarding party got aboard the sub, three cheers had gone up from the Nazis, who were then in the water. We found out later the Captain of the U-boat had ordered his men to give "three cheers for our sinking boat." He was convinced that his chart was clearly on its way to the bottom.

Though our maverick was now securely roped, she was not yet broken to the halter. She still wanted to circle or the right instead of towing meekly astern, the way tows are supposed to do. Before she would go our way, she sheered way out on the starboard quarter, drawing the towlines as taut as a fiddlestring.

I went aboard the sub myself about this time in response to a report that our boys had found a booby trap. I itched for an excuse to get over there and this was a legitimate one. I was an ordnance post graduate, knew more about fuses than anyone else in the ship, and so at the departure conference I had designated myself "officer in charge of booby traps," and had directed that no one else was to monkey with one.

I found the suspected trap attached to the watertight door of the after torpedo room, in such a manner that the door could not be opened without springing the trap. We had to get into that room to get at the hand steering gear because the sub's rudder was jammed hard over and we couldn't tow the U-boat properly until we got the rudder amidships.

Correct bomb disposal protocol called for clearing everyone else out of the boat while I operated on the suspected mechanism. However, the time was short and I didn't believe it actually was a booby trap; and besides that, it's nice to have company when you're doing a job like that. So with Earl Trosino and a couple of our boarders anxiously kibitzing, I carefully sprung the trap. The broad grins that spread across all faces as we got it open might well have been actuated by a mechanism on the trap. We eased the watertight door open, ready to slam it shut again if the torpedo room were flooded.

It was dry. So we hurried aft to the emergency steering gear and put the rudder amidships.

I don't know how many booby traps you must open before you're entitled to retire from the business. I was "certain" before I opened this one that it was not a booby trap, and it turned out I was right. I don't suppose anyone ever opens one unless he does think he is going to get away with it. But it's a racket that has no future in it, is bad for your ulcers, and I don't recommend it as a steady job.

While I tinkered around below, our hard-working painter had been busy on deck, rechristening our prize. When I climbed back out of the escape hatch I saw daubed in big red letters on the conning tower, her new name, "Can Do, Junior." We soon shortened this by dropping the first two words, and she has been "Junior" ever since to all hands in the task group.

This name, of course, harked back to that first order which we had handed to each new member of our crew as they stepped aboard in Astoria. We had called the *Guadalcanal* the *Can Do* ever since. Now, my bit of wishful thinking a year previously had produced a new name for one of Hitler's U-boats. Proving once again that when you hitch your wagon to a star almost anything can happen, including even finding an enemy U-boat hitched to your wagon by an inch and a quarter tow wire!

When I climbed the sea ladder again on the *Guadalcanal,* we hoisted the traditional broom at our masthead and squared away on a course for the nearest friendly port, Dakar. I cracked out a dispatch to Admiral Ingersoll telling him what we were doing and requesting a tanker and tug.

Within an hour we got a message back from Admiral Ingersoll, "Stay out of Dakar—proceed Bermuda."

This was a smart move because Dakar was a hotbed of international intrigue, teeming with Vichy French. If we had towed our prize into that nest of spies Berlin would have known all about it that same afternoon.

But Bermuda was seventeen hundred miles away and I was damned near out of fuel!

The sinking of the *Block Island* was still very fresh in our minds and I was in a little bit too much of a hurry to get the hell out of the area. During the night we steamed too fast and parted our towline. We had to patrol around the sub all night under a full moon, right smack in the middle of the U-boat lane from Cape Town to Cherbourg, while we roused up our two-and-a-quarter-inch wire from the boatswain's locker.

At the crack of dawn, there was a brisk breeze blowing, and at times we had to go ahead full on one engine and back full on the other to hold the ship in place as we again came alongside the sub. The working party handling the towline on the heaving, slippery deck of the U-boat had a nip and tuck struggle to get the cumbersome wire through the bull nose in the bow. It was a tough, dangerous job, a job for real seamen. Most of the lads on the sub's forecastle that morning had been apprentice seamen until just before joining the *Guadalcanal*. They proved themselves real seamen now.

For the next three days and nights we conducted flight operations with the sub in tow, and with very little wind across the flight deck on account of our slow speed. Admiral King thought I was gilding the lily when I told him about it later, and insisted on seeing the movies to prove it. This was another one of these "impossible" things which we found out you just take in your stride when the chips are down.

Earl Trosino put the heat on me to let him and his gang start the engines on the *U-505* and bring her in under her own power. Looking back on it now, I wish I had let them do it. But at the time I was afraid they might open the wrong valve and lose her—so we towed her in. I hereby apologize to Earl and his boys for grossly underestimating their capabilities.

People often ask me if we had anyone in our boarding parties who was an expert on submarines. The answer is "Yes." We had one man who had been a yeoman on one of our own submarines five years previously. So he could have told us anything we wanted to know about the paper work, correspondence, or filing system of submarines. But Earl Trosino was an expert on marine machinery whether it is installed in the *Queen Mary,* a harbor tug, or a submarine.

Trosino saved the sub after David captured it. All of Earl's previous training had been as chief engineer of a Sun Oil tanker. He had never been aboard a submarine before, but to him machinery is machinery, no matter what kind of a craft it is installed in. He spent hours crawling around under the floor plates of that foundering sub, tracing out pipe lines and closing the right valves to keep her afloat. He made no mistakes. If he had, he would have been trapped under the floor plates and would have gone down with her. (I recommended him for the Navy Cross, but all he got was the Legion of Merit.)

On the fourth day we turned our tow over to the fleet tug, *Abnaki,* which, together with a tanker, broke off from an eastbound convoy in response to orders from Admiral Ingersoll.

That tanker, the *Kennebec,* coming over the horizon was one of the most beautiful ships I have ever seen. To most of the task group she looked like an ordinary fat old tanker, but to me she was an angel from heaven. I had shaved things too closely on our fuel supply. I was on the verge of running out of oil and achieving a place in naval history comparable to the Foolish Virgins in the Bible!

Maybe there is something that could make a skipper look more ridiculous than running out of oil in the middle of the ocean, but I don't know what it is! Thank God I didn't have to try and explain *that* to Admiral Ingersoll.

The *Abnaki's* orders had simply told her to rendezvous with our task group "for a towing job." I solemnly scolded her skipper for jumping to the conclusion that the *Guadalcanal* had been hit and that he was going to tow *us* home.

You could hardly blame the *Abnaki* for failing to read between the lines of her orders correctly. I found out later that our first terse radio report of the capture was greeted with incredulity in London and Washington. The front offices suspected the communication officers of careless decoding on that word, "captured," because you just don't do that to modern ships in the 20th Century. As soon as they realized it was true, a super-duper *Top Secret* label was clamped on the news.

After the *Abnaki* took over the tow, Earl Trosino had an inspiration. "Junior" was still in a precarious state of nearly neutral buoyancy and we couldn't be sure we wouldn't lose her due to a slow leak. By this time Earl had traced all the drainage lines on the sub and knew how to pump her out—if he only had power enough to run the pumps. The battery was completely discharged by now, and I wouldn't let him try to start the Diesels, either to drive the boat or to recharge batteries. So Earl disconnected the Diesels from the shafts, set the switches properly on the electric power distribution board and persuaded me to have the *Abnaki* tow all night at ten knots. This high speed made the propellers turn over, thus turning the sub's electric motors, on which Earl had set the switches for charging the batteries. The electric motors, now acting as generators, didn't know that the propellers, not the Diesels, were making them turn, so they performed as if everything were normal and recharged the batteries. Next day we used the electric pumps to bring her up to full surface trim, and our worries were over.

During our haul to Bermuda I made a little gesture which didn't cost me a nickel but which assures me of at least one vote for President, any time I want to run. I knew the skipper of the *Pillsbury* was probably worrying about a possible board of investigation, when he got back to the United States with his side ripped open and the forward engine room full of water. So I sent the *Pillsbury* the following signal:

"This is for your files in regard to the damage done to your ship on June 4. Damage was done executing my orders and I assume responsibility."

A few days later I visited the badly wounded German skipper down in our sick bay. He was a totally different sort of character from Henke. Because of his wounds, he hadn't actually witnessed the capture, and he wouldn't believe that we had his U-boat in tow until I sent over to the sub and got a picture of his wife and kids from his cabin. Then he became greatly concerned about what would happen to him when he got back to Germany after the war. He conceded that the Nazis would lose the war, but he kept reiterating, "I will be punished for this."

The unwounded prisoners occupied the guest quarters which we had assigned to our prisoners from the *U-515* on the previous cruise. I was a bit uneasy about these guests.

The first impulse of a young American sailor when you get a bunch of prisoners aboard is to make friends with them and treat them generously. I don't believe in mistreating prisoners, but I was leary of these Nazis submariners. Fifty desperate men, who are willing to get hurt trying, could come very close to capturing a ship from a friendly bunch of youngsters. I kept reminding my people that such a reversal of the tables was no more improbable than the job that we had done on the *U-505*.

I almost threw a fit the first day we had these prisoners aboard when I saw one of my brave young guards, who must have thought he was Hopalong Cassidy, walk through the prisoners' cage carrying a tommy-gun. He was outnumbered thirty to one by the prisoners. At an earlier stage of the war, when the Nazis were still winning it, that lad would have been overwhelmed, and half a minute later our watch on the bridge would have been looking into the business end of that gun. But this U-boat crew let him get away with it that time, and never had another chance like that handed to them.

Another American impulse which we had to check was that of souvenir hunting. Even though comparatively few of our people had been aboard the sub, and even though they had been busy with important work while on board, I knew that a few souvenirs had been collected.

Before reaching Bermuda I addressed the crew one night at the movies on the subject of security. I pointed out that if we kept this capture secret, it could be one of the turning points of the war. We now had five of the acoustic torpedoes which had been raising hell with our ships. Our technical people would soon know how to counter them. But much more important than that, we had the Nazi code books and it was absolutely vital to prevent word of this capture from reaching Germany, because they would immediately change the code if it did.

I could see that the boys all went along with me a hundred per cent on this. Then came the gimmick in my talk. "There is no use whatsoever in having a souvenir unless you can show it around and brag about it. So, all those having souvenirs turn them in tomorrow to the Exec's Office and no questions will be asked. If souvenirs are found in anyone's possession after tomorrow, no questions will be asked, either—but the boom will be lowered!"

Next day the Exec's Office was inundated with the damnedest collection of junk you've ever seen. I don't see how the boys had time to close valves, pull wires off time bombs, struggle with towlines, and still collect that mountain of stuff. I know most of them would rather have turned in their right hands than those Lügers, binoculars, clocks, cameras, and officers' caps.

However, I'm very proud of the fact that our great secret was well preserved. As soon as those code books that we got out of the *U-505* arrived in Washington, our experts put a regular watch on the Nazi U-boat frequencies and read their messages to subs at sea as if they were in plain English. Although the Nazis changed their codes periodically, the key to these changes was in the code books!

Sometimes spies bring in red-hot information on enemy intentions, which you are afraid to use because it may be a plant. The Nazis had the detailed minutes of conferences between F.D.R., Churchill and Stalin, soon after they met, but made no use of this top secret intelligence. The *U-505's* code books obviously were no plant, and we made full use of them.

When Germany surrendered we found that the German Admiralty carried the *U-505* on the books as "probably sunk," having been last heard from on June 3. This is a high tribute to the sense of responsibility of all hands in the task group, especially since we were all just chockablock with the best story of our lives when we got back to the United States.

The secret was so well-kept, in fact, that some of the histories of the war don't even mention it. The capture was put in a special category even in the Navy's top secret files, and was never included in the overall U-boat war statistics. So some of the historians working from the regular top secret files haven't found out about it, yet.

We were the cockiest bunch of so-an-so's who ever sailed the seas as we came into Bermuda with our prize in tow and the broom at our masthead. Of course *we* had always known that we were good—now there would be no further argument about it.

The feelings of all hands were expressed by one of my brave young lads on June 6, just two days after our capture, when the long-awaited invasion of France began. As communiqués from SHAEF began to come in over the radio, telling about the thousands of ships and hundreds of thousands of men hitting the beaches in Normandy, we posted them on the bulletin boards. One of my modest young sailors skimmed hastily through these historic dispatches, shoved his hat to the back of his head, and said, "Boy, oh boy, look what Eisenhower had to do to top us!"

During the long voyage home a favorite pastime was drawing up plans for *Junior's* future operations. The best one brought to my attention was as follows:

"Send a message to Germany, using the captured codes and the U-boat's own transmitter, saying the *U-505* has been crippled, but is heading for a lagoon on the African coast where she will repair the damage and then return to Germany. Then put an American submarine crew aboard and send her up the Altenfjord in Norway, making all proper recognition signals, to sink the *Tirpitz*."

As a professional naval officer I can point out several flaws in this plan. But after sailing in the *Can Do*, I will never again say that *anything* is impossible for the current generation of American sailors.

Another subject of discussion on the trip home was prize money. In the old days of privateering, the crew of a ship which brought in a prize all shared in the distribution of her spoils. By maritime law and Navy regulations which we had patterned after the British Navy, men-of-wars men too shared the value of any ship which they captured. Some of the old British Captains were more interested in capturing rich prizes than they were in doing less remunerative jobs of more military importance.

Several of my officers pointed out a section in our current regulations which could be interpreted as still authorizing payment of prize money. We estimated the *U-505's* value as being several million dollars, and visualized the possibility of getting fat checks from the Treasury as we dragged our booty home. But that jackpot was never divided up. We found out when we got home that about thirty years previously some nosey and officious Congressman had repealed the law on which that section of the regulations depended.

The task group arrived in Bermuda on June 19, and turned the *U-505* over to my friend, the Commandant. As related in a previous chapter, you can't enter the lagoon in Bermuda except in daytime, and when our task group steamed through the entrance with the *Abnaki* and "Junior" bringing up the rear, the news spread all over the island about as quickly as the word would go through the ship that Betty Grable was coming aboard wearing a cellophane sarong. I still don't see how the military censors were able to prevent the news from reaching the mainland for nearly a year, but they did.

As soon as we anchored, the Provost Marshal came aboard to initiate negotiation for taking custody of the prisoners. By direction from Washington they were to remain in Bermuda for the duration, isolated from all other prisoners.

I don't know what sort of negotiations the Provost Marshal had in mind, but so far as I was concerned all he had to do was to send out a boat and take the Heinies ashore—and the sooner the better. This rear area soldier was evidently quite taken aback by such a straightforward approach to the problem. I think he had an idea that I would propose a plan, he would make counter proposals, and then we would spend a couple of days considering all the angles of the question and working out a compromise.

I exercised great patience during the early part of our discussion, and finally persuaded him to send a signal ashore for a boat right away. While we were waiting for the boat he said: "Of course I can only take the enlisted men today. We didn't have much notice of this, and the officers' section of our prison camp isn't ready yet."

Those feather merchants on duty at the Naval Operating Base, Bermuda, had known for fifteen days that we were coming! But I kept my temper, and talked calmly and deliberately for the next five minutes. . . . I didn't change my expression, or raise my voice.

I pointed out to the Provost Marshal that they had had two weeks' notice about our impending arrival, whereas we, on the ship, had only fifteen minutes warning of the unscheduled descent of our guests upon us—but we hadn't turned them away on that account. I compared the relative sizes of his millionaire's playground of an island and our tiny little ship.

It began to dawn on the Provost Marshal that he was dealing with an extremely difficult and narrow-minded individual, utterly incapable of grasping the broad problems which the security officer of a great island must consider.

I launched into a critical examination of his concepts of global strategy and found them unsound in many respects. I expressed veiled doubts about his ancestry, and wound up by making some very pessimistic and unpleasant predictions as to his future when he departed this vale of tears in which we live and began his life in the hereafter.

I didn't use a single four-letter word which I couldn't have used in talking to a Mother Superior, but, by the time I got through, that sandblasting which I had gotten from his boss six months before had been passed down the line with interest, in accordance with long established military custom.

As soon as his boat came alongside he bundled the prisoners—officers and all—into the boat and scrammed off of that ship, tumbling down the gangway two steps at a time as he left.

Upon arrival in the United States, I presented a book, which we found in the skipper's cabin of the *U-505*, to Admiral King. It's title was *Roosevelt's Kampf*. It was full of propaganda alleging that the United States was out to conquer the world. Admiral King presented the book to the President, together with our letter dedicating our capture to: "The principal character in the book, our Commander in Chief, the President."

The President took time out from the business of State

Bermuda, B.W.I.,

June 19, 1944.

Received from Commander E. Trosino, U.S.N.R.
(representing Captain D. V. Gallery, U.S.N.)
the German submarine U-505 which was captured at
sea by Task Group 22.3.

Signed _W. N. Christensen_

Rank _Comdr U.S.N._

Representing _Comnober_

to make the following reply, signed in his own hand. (See reproduction of letter on 220.)

This, incidentally, is the only official letter I have ever seen in which the President used his title as Commander in Chief of the Armed Forces.

For capturing the *U-505*, the task group later received the coveted Presidential Unit Citation. Thus, in less than a year, we rode to glory on the coattails of our star, and reached the goal we had set for ourselves on the day we went in commission.

At first the Board of Awards in Washington turned down Admiral Ingersoll's recommendation that the task group be given the P.U.C. They said the P.U.C. was a combat award, and the fact that nobody got killed on our side in the *U-505* action proved it wasn't much of a fight! Admiral King disdainfully overruled this verdict and personally ordered award of the P.U.C.

I made it a practice whenever any of our plank owners were detached to call them up to the cabin, hand them their orders in person, and wish them luck on their new assignment. Right after we got back to Norfolk from this cruise a tough little guy from Brooklyn came in to take his departure. He was obviously ill at ease and tongue-tied in the august precincts of the cabin. As I handed him his orders and pay accounts I said "Well, son, she turned out to be a pretty good ship after all, didn't she?"

He relaxed and grinned from ear to ear. A rough approximation of his uninhibited and unprintable reply, "No stuff, Cap'n."

The *Guadalcanal* was decommissioned and put in moth balls after the war. I went aboard her in 1948 and I'm sorry I did. Perhaps she wasn't dead, but she was sleeping very soundly. Her hangar deck was full of ghosts, and I prefer to remember her as she was in her heyday patrolling the sea lanes of the Atlantic.

I said earlier in the book that when a ship is put in commission all members of her crew loan her a piece of their souls, "to keep as long as they serve in her." I left that piece of mine with the *Guadalcanal* permanently.

As I look back on her now, I say with heartfelt gratitude, she was a good ship, she had a stout crew, and we had a bright star to steer her by.

NOTE: This book was written in 1950.

Since then the *U-505* has been brought up the St. Lawrence Seaway to Chicago, hauled out of the water, and installed on concrete cradles alongside the Museum of Science and Industry.

The *Guadalcanal* was taken out of mothballs, towed to Japan, and broken up for scrap in 1959.

August 19, 1944.

8 2061

From:	The Commander in Chief.
To :	Captain D. V. Gallery, U.S.N.,
	Commander Task Group 22.3 and
	Commanding Officer, U.S.S. GUADALCANAL.
Via :	The Commander in Chief, U.S. Fleet.
Subject:	Book Taken from the Captain's Bunk in the
	German Submarine U-505.'

    1.   I have received the book forwarded by your
letter of June 15, 1944, and I have noted with great
interest its remarkable history. It will be added to
the Library at Hyde Park and will serve as a lasting
testimonial of the enterprise, valor and determination
of you and your fine task group.

    2.   Please extend to all of your command my
thanks for your fine service to our country and for
your thought of me.

Franklin D. Roosevelt

EPILOGUE

Much water has gone under the bridge since the deeds recorded in this book were done. After smashing the unholy alliance of the Nazis and Japs we dumped the job of keeping peace on earth into the lap of the United Nations, and tossed our Armed Forces into the ash can. For a couple of years we lived in a fool's paradise thinking we could compromise with an even greater evil than the one we had just exterminated.

We did not see eye to eye with the Communists in all things, but they were our gallant allies and could do no wrong. Some of our bubbleheaded citizens saw only the flaws in our system, and none of the ugly cancers in the communist creed. They thought we had much to learn from the Reds, and could live happily with them forever after.

I trust we have learned enough about them now. The Iron Curtain has been slammed down on Poland, Czechoslovakia and the satellite countries. Our former allies would have starved us out of Berlin, except for the miracle of the airlift. Communist stooges have made a farce of deliberations in the United Nations. The fuse that leads to atomic explosions and World War III is burning briskly. By now it is obvious even to the bubbleheads that we exorcised one set of devils from the earth in 1945 only to make room for another equally evil horde. The last state of the world is no better than the first.

Meantime long-haired "experts" and eminent crackpots told us that even if war did come again, atom bombs, jet aircraft and guided missiles would make it an impersonal mechanical business that would be over in forty-eight hours. Technicians in underground command posts would control our atomic missiles with batteries of push buttons, and it would all be very scientific. Sailors and marines would play little part in such a war.

But on June 25, 1950, many of our befuddled citizens woke up with their usual Sunday morning hangover and found Korea leering at them. A lot of pipe dreams went down the scuppers in the next few months. The push buttons were put back on the laboratory shelves. Veteran ships which the soothsayers earmarked for the scrap heap were dragged out of moth balls in the back channels, recommissioned and rushed off to war again. From our rapidly narrowing foothold in Korea the old familiar cry went up: "For God's sake, send the Marines!"

While science was revolutionizing warfare, it had done nothing to revolutionize human nature. Man learns to control every force in nature except the evil within himself, so we are now confronted by the worst evil that man, with all his experience at it, has ever been able to produce.

Our way of life and communism's clash on many issues. We believe in free enterprise, freedom of speech, and the rights and dignity of the individual. The Communists do not. However, even these fundamental and far reaching differences might conceivably be reconciled and compromised.

But there is one difference on which no compromise is possible. We profess to believe in and worship God. The motto of our country is: "In God We Trust." The Communists deny the very existence of God. They are trying, by every devilish means at their disposal, to stamp out His memory and obliterate His name behind the Iron Curtain. This is one issue which can never be adjusted by peaceful, brotherly compromise. It is the real issue from which all the others stem. So long as it exists, our soldiers, sailors, marines and airmen will have bloody work to do every now and then. We had better remember that the Lord helps those who help themselves. We have no right to expect Him to pass a miracle for us every time our stupidity gets us into a jam.

At the present moment the U.S. is aroused, mobilization is underway, and before long we will be strong again.

But I'm afraid that we will remain strong only as long as we are scared. Pious wishful thinking throughout the country and political expediency can wreck our defenses again, just like they were wrecked after VJ day, and as no enemy assault has ever been able to wreck them. All that our enemies have to do to gain back the ground they are losing is to become sweet and reasonable for a brief interval, agree to anything we propose, and sign any piece of high-level gobbledegook which the diplomats draw up. They can put this country to sleep again in six months.

I have no confidence whatever in the possibility of preserving peace by making pacts with godless nations. I doubt the ability of our older generation to salvage the victory of World War II by practical, realistic and peaceful means.

I see only one star for us to steer by now. I *am* confident that so long as our way of life produces the kind of youth I served with in World War II, we will never lose a war on the battlefield. The grim truth which the older generation should ponder is that the safety of this country depends on the kids who are in high school now. When their elders bitch the works and explode the world, they are the ones who will have to pull the chestnuts out of the atomic fire.

These kids were in the fifth and sixth grades when I served with their elder brothers as set forth in these pages. The victory which their brothers won has turned to ashes, but fortunately for us oldsters, the new recruit now joining the fighting services is just as good as the men I've been writing about. They too are a "can do" generation.

So long as we keep our atomic powder dry, and raise our children to fear God, we need fear no other power on earth.

NOTE: Many of the kids I speak of above are now (1967) fighting in Vietnam. They are living up to what I said of them.